Britain's Hidden Role in the Rwandan Genocide

Britain's Hidden Role in the Rwandan Genocide examines the role of Great Britain as a global elite bystander to the crime of genocide, and its complicity, in violation of international criminal laws during the Rwandan genocide of 1994. As prevailing accounts confine themselves to the role and actions of the United States and the United Nations, the full picture of Rwanda's genocide has yet to be revealed. Hazel Cameron demonstrates that it is the unravelling of the criminal role and actions of the British that provides a more detailed answer to the question of 'why' the genocide in Rwanda occurred. In this book, she provides a systematic and detailed analysis of the policies of the British Government towards civil unrest in Rwanda throughout the 1990s that culminated in genocide. Utilising documentary evidence obtained as a result of Freedom of Information requests to the Foreign and Commonwealth Office, as well as material obtained through extensive interviews – with British Government Cabinet members, diplomats, Ambassadors to the United Nations Security Council, prisoners in Rwanda convicted of being leaders and organisers of genocide, and victims and survivors of genocide in Rwanda – the author finds that the actions of the British and French governments, both before and during the Rwandan genocide of 1994, were disassociated from human rights norms. It is suggested that the decision-making of the Major Government during the period 1990–94 was for the advancement of the interrelated goals of maintaining power status and ensuring economic interests in key areas of Africa.

This account of the legal culpability of the powerful within the corridors of government, in both London and Paris, shows that these behaviours cannot be conceptualised under existing notions of state crime. This book serves to illuminate the inadequacies and limitations of a concept of state crime in international law as it currently stands, and will be of considerable interest to anyone concerned with the misuse of state power.

Hazel Cameron is a Lecturer in the School of International Relations at the University of St Andrews. She is affiliated to the International State Crime Initiative (ISCI) based at King's College London in association with Harvard University and the University of Hull.

Britain's Hidden Role in the Rwandan Genocide

The Cat's Paw

Hazel Cameron

Routledge
Taylor & Francis Group
a GlassHouse Book

First published 2013
by Routledge
2 Park Square, Milton Park, Abingdon, Oxon OX14 4RN

Simultaneously published in the USA and Canada
by Routledge
711 Third Avenue, New York, NY 10017

A GlassHouse book

Routledge is an imprint of the Taylor & Francis Group, an informa business

British Library Cataloguing in Publication Data
A catalogue record for this book is available from the British Library

Library of Congress Cataloging in Publication Data
Cameron, Hazel.
Britain's hidden role in the Rwandan genocide : the Cat's paw / Hazel Cameron.
p. cm.
Includes bibliographical references.
1. Genocide–Rwanda. 2. Responsibility to protect (International law) 3. Principals (Criminal law) 4. Genocide intervention. 5. Genocide–Prevention. I. Title.
KTD454.C36 2013
967.57104'31–dc23
2012002356

ISBN 978-0-415-61960-8 (hbk)
ISBN 978-0-415-53339-3 (pbk)
ISBN 978-0-203-11359-2 (ebk)

Typeset in Times New Roman
by Taylor & Francis Books

To my Mum and Dad, Margaret and Scott Cameron, and all of my loved ones who have gone on to a better life.

Contents

Acknowledgements

This study was supported by the Carnegie Trust for the Universities of Scotland, a private charitable trust endowed by Andrew Carnegie (1835–1919), the Scottish-American industrialist who became one of the most important philanthropists of his era. The Carnegie Trust for the Universities of Scotland has an 'ambitious programme of philanthropy' and 'respect for the Scottish tradition of learning'. I am immensely grateful to the Carnegie Trust for the award of a doctoral scholarship and several small research grants, without which this study would not have been possible. My first visit to Rwanda was, however, funded by the Andrew J Williamson Memorial Trust, generously supported by Joyce Williamson in memory of her son who died tragically in a car accident whilst a student of politics at the University of Stirling in 1981.

I would like to take this opportunity to thank the victims, survivors, witnesses and perpetrators of genocide who I met in Rwanda and beyond, who generously shared their time and testimonies with me. This includes those witnesses I met in the mountains of Bisesero, Rwanda, whose voices are found in this book as promised. I would also like to thank the respondents of this study in the West who kindly granted interviews and provided me with a unique insight into the politics and ethical challenges of decision-making.

I am indebted to David Whyte, University of Liverpool, for his tremendous encouragement, inspiration and support in his role of PhD supervisor. It has been an amazing privilege to benefit from such an enthusiastic and inspirational mentor. Thanks also to Penny Green, Sandra Walklate, Cathy Taylor, Graeme Young, and Sam Punch for academic support. It is also important that I acknowledge my heartfelt appreciation for the wonderful staff I encountered at the University of Stirling library over the years who were always willing to provide assistance with a smile. Many thanks to Ian Taylor, University of St Andrews, for his support and encouragement in my new career at the University of St Andrews, and his invaluable feedback on a draft of the manuscript. All errors, of course, remain mine alone.

I wish to give credit and thanks to professional photographer Kipp Baker, Fort Worth, Texas, for kindly allowing me copyright of an image of his cat, 'Pancho', displayed on the front cover of this book. Sadly, Pancho passed away in November 2009.

Finally, thanks to all my family and friends for your love and support through good times and bad. You know who you are.

The Cat's Paw Explained

The cat's paw is a phrase derived from Jean de La Fontaine's fable, 'The Monkey and the Cat' (French title, *Le Singe et le Chat*), which appeared in the second edition of his *Fables Choisies* in 1679. There are popular idioms derived from it in both English and French (e.g. a cat's paw) with the general meaning of being a tool or a dupe of another. The allusion is to the fable of the monkey who wanted to get some roasted chestnuts from the fire, and uses the cat's paw to get them from the hot ashes.

Acronyms

APC	Armored Personnel Carrier
AU	African Union
BBTG	Broad-Based Transitional Government
CIA	Central Intelligence Agency
CND	Conseil National de Développement
DAMI	Détachement d'assistance militaire et d'instruction
DMI	Department of Military Intelligence
DPKO	Department of Peacekeeping Operations
DRC	Democratic Republic of Congo
FAR	Forces Armées Rwandaises (Rwanda Armed Forces)
FCO	Foreign and Commonwealth Office
GOR	Government of Rwanda
ICISS	International Commission on Intervention and State Sovereignty
ICJ	International Court of Justice
ICRC	International Committee of the Red Cross
ICTR	International Criminal Tribunal for Rwanda
ICTY	International Criminal Tribunal for the Former Yugoslavia
ILC	International Law Commission
MDR	Mouvement Démocratique Républicain
MRND	Mouvement Révolutionnaire National Pour le Développement
NRA	National Resistance Army
OAU	Organization of African Unity
Parmehutu	Parti du movement de l'émancipation des Bahutu
R2P	Responsibility to Protect
RANU	Rwandan Alliance for National Unity
RPF	Rwandan Patriotic Front
RTLM	*Radio et Télévision Libres des Milles-Collines*
SAM	Surface-to-Air Missile
SIS	Secret Intelligence Service
SRSG	Special Representative of the Secretary-General
SZH	Safe Humanitarian Zone
UKMIS NY	United Kingdom Mission to the United Nations

UNAMIR	United Nations Assistance Mission for Rwanda
UNGC	United Nations Convention on the Prevention and Punishment of the Crime of Genocide
UNOMUR	United Nations Observer Mission Uganda–Rwanda
UNSC	United Nations Security Council

Preface

On arrival at the entrance to the prison in Kigali, my immediate access was restricted by a mere length of rope that was lowered by the guard on duty on production of my official letter of authority to enter. Thereafter I was left to wander down the sloping pathway and into the courtyard of the prison, where crowds of family and friends of those incarcerated gathered to hand in food for the inmates' lunch. I was not entirely alone as the Government insisted on providing me with an 'interpreter' named Emmanuel, despite having made my own arrangements with an independent translator. Emmanuel was, of course, not an interpreter but a member of Rwandan intelligence, and I was strongly advised by a friend in Rwanda to be very careful.

Despite being within the grounds of an overcrowded Rwandan prison with several hundred prisoners in identical pink uniforms milling around and no sign of prison guards in attendance, at no time was there any sense of danger. The atmosphere within the prison was one of cordiality between the prisoners, prison governor and the prison guards – on the rare occasions they were seen. This air of geniality was unanticipated in an environment where a vast number of those present have been charged or convicted of crimes of extreme violence and multiple deaths.

I had been granted an interview with Agnes Ntamabyariro, a former Judge who was the Minister of Justice in the interim government in Rwanda formed in April 1994 after the assassination of President Habyarimana. Ntamabyariro fled to Zambia with her family in 1994; the following year, she was drugged and kidnapped by Rwandan commandoes, awakening to find herself in prison in Kigali. When I met her more than a decade later, she was still awaiting trial, accused of being one of the leaders and organisers of the 1994 genocide, responsible for crimes against humanity and genocide. She was sentenced to life imprisonment in January 2009, although there is doubt over the credibility of the prosecution witnesses at her trial. Ntamabyariro is the only member of the former government to be tried in Rwanda. The prosecution have requested that she be held in isolation for the duration of her sentence.

Her advice to me was, 'Look at the British – they are guiltier than the French'.

As I left the prison and stepped over the lowered length of rope that marked my exit, the air of geniality of the past few hours quickly dissipated.

Chapter 1

An Introduction

In an ideal world, states would be able to keep politics and economics apart. But states are political and politics inevitably encroach on economics in the pursuit of international objectives. Critical criminologists have successfully demonstrated that states can be crucial in the organisation and support of activities that violate their own laws and international laws, and in so doing fulfil their own broader political and economic objectives (see Coleman *et al.* 2009). International criminal law pertinent to genocide is a useful example of the aforementioned, and is employed in this book to provide a lens for understanding the scope of liability relative to state complicity in genocide where the state under examination is not the primary perpetrator or co-author of the massacres. This is particularly relevant in an era when certain states have substantially greater power and resources than others and seek to influence events abroad.

Colonialism and genocide

There is no indication as to where or when the first genocide occurred since the evidence from antiquity is contradictory, ambiguous or missing, but it is fair to say that the crime is ancient. Accounts are available of horrifying genocidal massacres in the eighth and seventh centuries BC in the Assyrian empire, as well as the many genocidal conflicts in the Bible and the chronicles of Greek and Roman historians.

Charles Darwin drew analogies between genocide and the colonial world, arguing that 'wherever the European has trod, death seems to pursue the aboriginal' (cited in Merivale 1861: 541). Some of Darwin's first diary entries note his observations of European colonists doing their best to make the indigenous people extinct. Deliberate colonial policies promoting genocide and the elimination of a culture cannot, however, be described as a universal feature of colonialism (Kuper 1981; Thomas 1994; Mann 2005), although European colonisers undoubtedly largely displayed a wilful disregard for the fate of the colonised. Such was the case in sixteenth-century Mexico, where Spanish colonists inadvertently introduced disease, reducing a population of over 5 million in 1492 to only 500,000 by 1892, with survivor figures deteriorating even further to 250,000 by 1900. That the substantial loss of life in indigenous communities came about accidentally or as a result of callousness as opposed to intent to kill does not lessen the culpability of the colonisers (Sale 1990; Stannard 1992; Gellately and Kiernan 2003).

The introduction of disease by colonising forces was not always unintentional. Throughout the seventeenth and eighteenth centuries, the colonies that became the United States saw massive brutality and deliberate exterminations for which European forces must bear responsibility (Gellately and Kiernan 2003). Levene argues that their conduct is describable as genocide (2005b). It was a British army officer who, in 1763, urged a field officer in Philadelphia to deliberately introduce smallpox amongst the tribes of disaffected American Indians, suggesting the use of infected hospital blankets to inoculate the intended victims, 'as well as to try Every other method that can serve to extirpate this Execrable Race [sic]'. The orders of one army officer to his troops was to 'Kill and scalp all, little and big … Nits make lice' (Stannard 1992: 129). Military hospital records confirm that infected blankets and handkerchiefs were removed and further documents reveal 'the eruption of epidemic smallpox' among Delaware and Shawnee Indians in the vicinity, at about the same time the blankets were distributed (Fenn 2000: 1554–8).

In the late eighteenth and early nineteenth centuries the two most notable repeat-perpetrators of genocide were Britain and the United States. Such instances of genocide would appear to relate closely to regions on their domestic or colonial frontiers where state consolidation remained incomplete, or where expansion continued to be contested by native people (Levene 2005a: 162). The 'complete eradication of the autochthonous element [the native Tasmanians] in the seventy years after the first white settlement on the south Australian island, in 1803, has been repeatedly taken as a unique example of a British organised genocide' (Levene 2005b: 37). Whilst some comparative genocide scholars view the Tasmanian case as one of unmitigated genocide (see Kuper 1981; Fein 1993), the majority of Australian experts are considerably more circumspect in their analysis (see Ryan 1996: 3; Moses 2000: 103).

The Irish Famine of 1846–51 killed a million people in peacetime, and led to the enforced migration of a further million people from another British colony:

> What happened in Ireland in the early 1650s … is recognisably akin to the 'dirty' counter-insurgency wars of the twentieth century where an imperial or colonial power, or its proxies, seeks to win a struggle against an alternative political programme by treating not just the insurgents but their whole supporting population as equally guilty and thereby equally expendable.
>
> (Levene 2005b: 55)

It is generally accepted that the British Government provided minimal assistance to the starving Irish, and none at all after October 1847. Indeed,

1849 witnessed the British Prime Minister Russell refuse Ireland the £100,000 that was considered necessary to prevent further starvation (Ó Gráda 1999: 77, 83). Some commentators argue that such conduct is perceivable as a British 'policy of extermination of the Irish' (Gellately and Kiernan 2003: 25), however not all scholars agree that genocide took place in Ireland at the hands of the British Government (Kuper 1981; Ó Gráda 1999: 10).

The Herero were probably the first ethnic group subjected to genocide in the twentieth century. The slaughter of the Herero by the German rulers of South West Africa (now the Independent Republic of Namibia) from 1904 onwards was amongst the most destructive of the reprisals of colonisers against colonized in punishment for rebellion (Pakenham 1992: 602–15; Bridgman and Worley 2004: 15–52; Sarkin 2009). Lau (1989: 4–5, 8) raises many provocative questions about the Herero tragedy, arguing that the Herero were not victims of genocide, rather victims of 'a successful psychological warfare, never followed in deed' (ibid: 5). However this has been vigorously and effectively contradicted by Dedering (1993). The current consensus of genocide scholars is that the Herero *were* subjected to an officially sanctioned colonial genocide policy (see Drechsler 1980; Bridgman and Worley 2004; Gewald 2004; Hull 2005) although politicians remain reluctant to classify this tragedy as such whenever possible (Schaller 2005: 532). In 2001, using the procedures of the Alien Torts Claim Act of 1789 in a US federal court, the Herero became the first ethnic group to seek reparations from Germany and certain named companies, for war crimes committed overseas, including colonial policies that fit the definition of genocide (Gewald 2004: 60; Cooper 2007: 113–20; Sarkin 2009).

It has been argued that Joseph Conrad's *Heart of Darkness* is the most enduring and powerful literary indictment of imperialism in Africa (Watt 1979: 161), where colonialism stands accused of torture, cruelty and encouraging cannibalism in King Leopold's Congo Free State (Morel 1905: 437–52).[1] In the meantime, Hochschild's *King Leopold's Ghost* (1999) has significantly influenced contemporary public discussion of European atrocities committed in the Congo. He maintains that although the 'killing in the Congo was of genocidal proportion' it cannot be considered a 'real' genocide, since King Leopold's aim was not the extermination of all the Congolese or of any particular tribes in the Congo (ibid: 2, 25). This is contrary to the view of Raphael Lemkin, a Polish Jewish specialist in international law and the founding figure of the United Nations Convention oin the Prevention and Punishment of Genocide (UNGC). In his unpublished material, Lemkin argues that 'the imposition of Belgian colonial rule in the Congo and the forced labour of the indigenous population that went with it was an unambiguous genocide' (Schaller 2005: 535). Clearly Lemkin believed that Leopold *did* attempt to exterminate particular tribes in the Congo. It should be noted that, although Lemkin was very much against the violent suppression of the Herero by the Germans and the monstrous exploitation of the Congo by the

Belgians, the founder of the UNGC was in fact 'an enthusiastic advocate of colonialism' and somewhat surprisingly, had himself an extremely racist perception of Africans, whom he described as 'either weak-willed and helpless victims' or as 'bloodthirsty cannibals' (ibid: 536).

Many of Lemkin's unpublished works deal with the atrocities committed by European colonialists (ibid: 531), and indeed colonialism is central to Lemkin's concept of genocide. McDonnell and Moses have detailed how 'the intellectual breakthrough that led to the concept of genocide' came as a direct result of Lemkin's interest in colonial genocides, and not, as is commonly believed, as a response to the Holocaust (ibid: 501). They argue that the colonial foundation to the coining of the term 'genocide' has been 'studiously ignored in the literature' and is only now emerging as a theme in studies of imperial history (ibid: 502).

In a 1941[1] BBC radio broadcast, the British Prime Minister Winston Churchill described the actions of the Nazis in Europe as 'a crime without a name' (Power 2002: 29; Elder 2005: 470). Two years later, Lemkin created the neologism of 'genocide' to express, 'the use or a user of deliberate, systematic measures such as killing, bodily or mental injury, unliveable conditions, prevention of births, calculated to bring about the extermination of a racial, political, or cultural group or to destroy the language, religion, or culture of a group' (Elder 2005: 469).

Contemporary genocide

In the spring of 1994, the impoverished country of Rwanda became international front-page news because of genocide. Rwanda is a small, rural, landlocked country in the Great Lakes region of central Africa with few natural resources and minimal industry, and with coffee and tea as its primary exports. The same is not true of its near neighbours, Uganda and the Democratic Republic of the Congo (DRC),[2] which are rich in raw materials. In common with numerous countries of the African continent, Rwanda has a history of racism and colonialism in its post-decolonisation era, and has witnessed violence, fear and corruption within its borders.

Throughout the early 1990s Rwanda experienced a low-intensity civil war between the Hutu-dominated Government of Rwanda (GOR) and the Tutsi-dominated Rwandan Patriotic Front (RPF). On the evening of 6 April 1994, the assassination of the President of Rwanda, Juvénal Habyarimana triggered violence against the Tutsi and moderate Hutu in Rwanda. Hundreds of thousands of Rwandans were massacred in the ensuing three months. All serious observers and certainly the international courts have universally declared that events of April to July 1994 in Rwanda constitute genocide as defined by the UNGC. In addition to those crimes committed by the Hutu populations are the mass murders and torture committed by the RPF throughout the 1990s and into the new millennium.

There is a consensus globally that the international community, including the United Kingdom, 'failed' Rwanda in 1994, but after 18 years of systematic disinformation there exists a collective ignorance about what information and intelligence the United Kingdom was in possession of, what options were available to them, and how they responded. This book explores the British government's political and military relationship with the RPF from its inception, throughout the civil war of Rwanda 1990–94 and the subsequent genocide. This permits us, for the first time, to establish Britain's role in the genocide, and to decide whether Britain indeed failed the people of Rwanda – and if so, how it failed them and what the British Government's motivation was in adhering to such policies in Africa.

With few exceptions, journalists and academics have sidelined these questions, assuming that, having no embassy in Rwanda, the British would have had no involvement in the policies relevant to this small country in the period 1990–94, apart from its role as a permanent member to the United Nations Security Council (UNSC). This overarching negation of Britain's role pervades, despite Britain also being a signatory to the UNGC. Where there is now a substantial body of literature detailing the roles of the US and French governments in Rwanda throughout the 1990s, there is no such scholarship to illuminate the role of the United Kingdom in the genocide. The original and rigorous research that forms the body of this book is the first analysis of British policy towards the civil war and subsequent genocide in Rwanda, and illuminates hitherto hidden relationships and findings that assist in pushing back the boundaries of the 'genocide template' (Lemarchand 2006: 9).

The book provides an examination of political life through an exploration of both official and unofficial documentation, as well as previously unavailable insights into the opinions and explanations of senior British politicians of the 1994 Conservative Government led by Sir John Major and members of the Foreign and Commonwealth Office (FCO) regarding Britain's response to the genocide in Rwanda.

Sources of evidence: documents

Many of the early sociologists such as Marx, Durkheim and Weber used documentary research in their studies. It continues to be an important stand-alone research tool and an invaluable part of most schemes of triangulation. Hughes (1996) points out that gaining access to documentary information while conducting criminological research is an ongoing process of negotiating and renegotiating, and this was the case in efforts to obtain official documentary evidence from both Oxfam UK and the FCO. Despite verbal assurances of unproblematic access to the Oxfam documentary archive in Oxford, access was refused after formal application, with no reason provided. It was only after a lengthy, dogged pursuit by letter, email and telephone that the requested documentation – namely, a copy of a letter that had been hand-delivered by its author, David Bryer, Director of Oxfam, to Prime Minister Major, highlighting his concerns that a genocide was taking place in Rwanda – was forthcoming and forwarded by the Oxfam archivist. Such reluctance to permit access to relevant documentation can perhaps in part be explained by a former Oxfam worker, who states:

> With a plethora of new organisations now in the lists, profile is all, and accentuating the positive becomes a 'must'. This is particularly important for those agencies that depend heavily on official funding, since governments want to support organisations that are doing highly visible work. Even an agency like Oxfam, which draws most of its long-term funding from the British general public, is far from immune to such pressures.
>
> (McIntosh 1997: 467)

In sharp contrast to the difficulty of accessing documents from Oxfam UK, the International Committee of the Red Cross (ICRC), unreservedly mailed all the requested documentation both timeously and free of charge.

Many of the most useful primary documents for the purposes of this study are defined as 'public records', being 'records of, or held in, any department of Her Majesty's Government in the United Kingdom' (Public Records Act 1958: c. 51); as such they fall under closure regulations usually of 30 years' duration, and are only accessible prior to this time if they fall to be disclosed within the Freedom of Information Act (FoI) 2000. Price (cited in Walters 2003: 104) has argued that 'fieldwork that relies on the Freedom of Information Act remains fraught with difficulties' due to the often lengthy periods involved in processing requests, and 'it is common that requested information is blacked-out on receipt'. An initial request to the FCO in London for release of documentation pertinent to this study was declined. After further, more specific applications, a rapport was established with a member of staff from the Africa Desk of the FCO, who proved sympathetic to the needs of the study and helpful in negotiating the release of appropriate documents where permissible. These included official cables and telexes dispatched between the FCO, the British embassies in Kinshasa, Kampala, Dar es Salaam, Washington, Paris and New York, and individual Cabinet ministers.[3] Despite this, however, a vast amount of significant documentary evidence remains classified by the FCO, disclosure being refused in terms of FoI. The reason provided for such refusal is the potential to jeopardise relations between the United Kingdom, France, Rwanda and Uganda. The written response explaining this decision is held by the author and has been noted in full below:

> We consider that the release of some of the information you are requesting would be likely to prejudice relations between the United Kingdom and other States under *Section 27 (1)(a) – International*

> *Relations – relations with another State.* This exemption requires the balance of the public interest test.
>
> (Letter in possession of author, 6 July 2006)

> While we acknowledge there is a public interest in the release of information on this subject we consider that release of these documents would, or would be likely, to prejudice the United Kingdom's relations with the Governments of Rwanda and Uganda. It is in the United Kingdom's interest to maintain a constructive relationship with these two countries so that we can fulfill our development obligations in the region. The release of information in a further document could also harm our international relations with France; France is a key United Kingdom ally and we would not want to put at risk United Kingdom-France cooperation in a number of areas. We have concluded therefore that the public interest in maintaining good relations with Rwanda, Uganda and France outweighs the public interest in disclosing the information.
>
> (Letter in possession of author, 7 September 2007)

This may be a legitimate reason for denying access to the requested information or alternatively it may be an 'orchestrated technique' to prevent the release of data, conduct that David Simon describes as a form of 'political deviance' (2002: 232).

Further documentary evidence analysed was in the form of relevant and reliable information and intelligence from both official and unofficial sources that were available to the British Government in 1990–94. Archives explored include the online Hansard archive, the online United Nations documentary archive and Nexis, all of which are in the public domain. A systematic search of the United Nations's online archive provided all the letters and reports of the UNSC President and all official letters, reports and statements of the UN Secretary-General for the relevant period.

Sources of evidence: interviews

In addition to documents, the research was dependent on interviews with elite and non-elite participants. The reality of modern democracy is that many political decisions are taken by small groups of highly qualified and knowledgeable individuals, and it is their shared assumptions and meanings that inform the private worlds which are explored in this study. Elites can be loosely defined as those in close proximity to power or policymaking, who have high access to knowledge, high status, high expressive ability and low accessibility. The powerful elite interviewees of this study are describable as actors in positions of power within the British Government, the United Nations and some of its organs. These range from British government ministers of the most senior level, to civil servants employed within the FCO at various levels of seniority, and key members of the UNSC of 1994. Some social scientists display an attitude of pessimism towards researching elites, arguing that 'the powerful are unwilling to cooperate, reticent to talk and protective of their privacy' (Williams 1989: 254). This was not the case in this study when the elite respondents were approached; to the contrary, there was an evident receptiveness to the study and a willingness to spend time discussing thoughts, views and observations, albeit in many respondents emanating from a desire to correct what they perceived as misconceptions of their responsibility for the genocide in Rwanda by failing to orchestrate a UN intervention to stop the genocide in April 1994.

The non-elite interviews were of equal significance to this study. Time spent by the author in Rwanda 2005–06 provided a rich insight into the experiences of some of the perpetrators of genocide held in Rwandan prisons, and many of the survivors and victims of the genocide, including those in the then insecure mountainous Bisesero region. The research resulted in the development of two substantively different data sets: the first data set pertained to the study of Britain's role in the Rwandan genocide; the second data set pertained to events in Bisesero in 1994 which revealed a valuable and somewhat remarkable sub-case study of the Rwandan genocide and the role of the French Operation Turquoise in Rwanda in 1994.

The approach undertaken for this study illuminates the complexities of the institution of international law as conditioned by modern politics. It further evidences that international politics and law is a relationship of fascinating intricacy and intrigue, which finds expression in such diverse areas as complicity in genocide. Indeed, juxtaposing the two datasets produces a complex and layered understanding of complicity in genocide. The research approached the concept of power in international politics from the perspective that powerful manipulation is not readily visible. Having stripped away layers of complexity, the research reveals how power operates in several dimensions, influenced by the underlying precepts of economic advantage, rather than human rights norms.

Criminology and genocide studies

In light of the increasing pervasiveness of genocide in the twentieth century, it is perhaps surprising that, until the 1970s, genocide studies tended to be the remit of historians and theologians, with social scientists rarely turning their attention to this particular type of criminality. Although a decade has passed since Yacoubian (2000) accused criminologists of paying little attention to genocide, there continues to be no specific criminological explanations applied to genocide, and sociological attention remains scant. This is despite genocide having been legally defined as a crime by the United Nations since the 1940s. According to Hagan *et al.* (2005), Raphael Lemkin, the 'founding father' of the UNGC, is barely known to today's criminologists.

Historically, criminology's main area of concern was conventional criminality with little attention devoted to the harm emanating from the misuse of political and economic power. However, the healthy growth of the study of state criminality in recent years is evident in several special issues dedicated to State Crime (*British Journal of Criminology* 45(4), 2005 and the *Journal of Critical Criminology* 17(1), 2009) and the 2012 launch of a new international peer-reviewed journal entitled *State Crime*.

The study of state criminality is by definition a political enterprise that includes the study of power, ideology, law, international treaties, and public and foreign policy. Although its inclusion in the field of criminology is indisputed, there remains a debate within criminology about the scope and subject matter of state crime, reflected in the polarity of definitions of the concept (see Green and Ward 2004). Humanistic criminologists have presented a definition of state crime whereby any institution in society that tolerates and/or promotes violations of human rights is criminal, irrespective of whether it is an individual, a corporation or the state that does the depriving (Schwendinger and Schwendinger 1975: 134). At the other end of the spectrum is Chambliss's legalistic approach, which limits conceptions of 'state organised crime' to 'acts defined by law as criminal, and committed by state officials in the pursuit of their job as representative of the state' (1989: 184). The use of international law provides a substantial framework for defining state crime, including as it does a solid legalistic foundation. Definitions of state crime are many, but this book limits its sphere of interest to those state criminal activities that are unambiguously in breach of international law. Historians, political scientists and international jurists have contributed greatly to understandings of international crime, but criminology can also provide an important contribution. This book utilises the concept of state crime to understand and respond to assertions of the international community's 'failure' in Rwanda, and as such potential crimes of complicity in genocide in terms of international criminal law.

By undertaking a socio-legal approach in the analysis of the available international criminal law pertinent to genocide, we are able to address the unavoidable socio-legal questions in the context of genocide and the influence of powerful institutions. Such an approach also highlights the limits of legal and academic understandings of genocide, the concept of complicity in genocide, and most particularly the concept of complicity as a bystander to genocide.

The criminological study discussed in this book provides an innovative lens for the crime of genocide in Rwanda, illuminating the responses, actions, motivations and ultimately the role of the powerful government actors of the United Kingdom, a nation external to the country of genocide but nonetheless a contracting party to the UNGC. A brief sub-case study of France, as previously mentioned, also permits us to explore the impact of colonialism on genocidal conflict with the objective of concluding whether the genocide of Rwanda in 1994 requires to be understood in terms of the country's colonial history. The study also permits us to question whether imperialism truly ended in Africa after the introduction of independence for the continent in the 1960s.

This book was inspired by the rigorous analytical research of Alison Des Forges, an African historian and human rights activist who, at the time of her sudden death on 12 February 2009, was the senior advisor for the African continent at Human Rights Watch. Her specialty was in the Great Lakes region of Africa, but she had a particular expertise in the 1994 Rwandan genocide, with a combined breadth of knowledge, clear analysis and depth of historical understanding otherwise unknown by any outside observer of Rwanda. As a result, she was able to draw strong conclusions from her careful and comprehensive consideration of the data. Her investigation, *Leave None to Tell the Story* (1999), is the most wide-ranging, thoroughly researched and reliable source of information on the 1994 genocide. The scope of Alison's research enabled her to see what the majority cannot, namely both sides of the genocidal coin, which includes cease-fire violations, human rights abuses, killings, and other abuses committed by the RPF before, during and after the genocide. The global focus has been on the crime of genocide in Rwanda. But those who fell victim to genocide in Rwanda in 1994 were not the only victims in the country. The RPF, which invaded Rwanda from Uganda in 1990 and went on to become the current Government of Rwanda, presided over by Paul Kagame, murdered tens of thousands of people in Rwanda. Des Forges was concerned that explanations of the genocide readily identified the Hutu of Rwanda as the protagonists of the mass atrocities, and did not take into account the violent mode of management, discriminatory practices and large numbers of civilians killed by the Tutsi-dominated RPF.

By employing a framework of state crime, it is my hope that this book produces a more complex and layered understanding of both sides of the genocide coin, in the spirit of Alison Des Forges. It is being published at a time of increasing interest in Britain's policy, both current and historical, towards Rwanda. It is also being completed during a period of diplomatic tension between the governments of Rwanda and Britain, the first time such a situation has arisen since the official agreements of cooperation between the two countries post-genocide. This tension is a result of the Metropolitan Police uncovering a plot by the Government of Rwanda to assassinate Rwandan nationals residing in London because of their political opposition to the regime of President Kagame. In contrast to the contemporary tension between London and Kagame, the book explores the hypothesis that the government of Uganda and indeed the RPF, were the cat's paw of the British Government in the period 1990–94.

Outline of the book

An open discussion of Western institutional complicity, facilitating a genuine and reflective debate, is imperative and encouraged. Having explored the historical interrelationship between colonialism and genocide, and the limited scholarly efforts to conceptualise compliance in such atrocities, we embark on the main focus of this book. Chapter 2 discusses the concept of 'the bystander' in general terms, and briefly engages in a socio-historical discussion of the development and implementation of international criminal law as both a body of proscriptive law and social control. This permits the development of the concept of what shall be thereafter termed the 'external global elite bystanders'. The exploration of international criminal law and complicity within this chapter provides a lens for understanding the scope of complicity and the liability of states as responsible actors in an age when certain states have substantially greater resources than others, and when powerful states seek to influence events abroad. It also furthers the development of the criminology of complicity in violations of international criminal law.

Chapter 3 details the historical, social, political and economic context of developments in Rwanda throughout the twentieth and late nineteenth centuries, exploring pre-colonial, colonial and independent Rwandan society in an effort to establish a narrative regarding ancient internal relationships and the impact of the socially constructed racist categories introduced by Rwanda's European colonisers.

Chapter 4 provides an overview of the societal and political developments in Rwanda over the previous two decades, highlighting both the formal and informal changes within the country, from late 1990 onwards, in response to the ongoing civil war between the RPF and the Rwandan Armed Forces (*Forces Armées Rwandaises*, FAR), which culminated in the assassination of President Habyarimana and genocide in 1994.

Chapter 5 endeavours to conceptualise complicity in genocide by a European colonialist state in a post-colonial era by exploring ongoing legal debates in relation to French complicity in the Rwandan genocide. This chapter outlines the post-independence political and military relationship that France nurtured with Rwanda, with a particular focus on the period from 1990 to the genocide of 1994. The actions of the UN-sanctioned French military Operation Turquoise are analysed by utilising a case study of the genocidal killings that took place in Bisesero, a mountainous area of Kibuye Prefecture in south-western Rwanda, and one of the few locations where the Tutsi inhabitants vigorously resisted the genocide. This chapter challenges the idea that French motives during the genocide were humanitarian, and argues that in June 1994 the French deliberately and effectively used a 'humanitarian intervention' as a cloak for the defence of narrow state interests, creating a protective corridor to facilitate the safe passage of fleeing génocidaires of the interim 'Hutu Power' government later characterised by the International Criminal Tribunal for Rwanda (ICTR) as controlling the genocide. The French intervention also facilitated the defeat of resistance in Bisesero, crushing the few remaining survivors on the mountainsides. Interviews with survivors of Bisesero, former Hutu militiamen and former Rwandan soldiers reveal how French soldiers continued to provide the militia with training, arms and indoctrination into hate ideologies throughout the genocide, and in some instances actively participated in the killing of Tutsis. The detailed analysis of such case material clearly evidences instances of French state criminality whose actions as an external global elite bystander to genocide can be said to have assisted, aided or abetted the perpetrators of genocide in Rwanda in numerous ways. This analysis also substantiates the necessity of understanding events in Rwanda in terms of colonialism, as previously determined in Chapter 2 herein.

Chapter 6 examines the British Government's political and military relationship with the RPF from its inception in 1986, and throughout the period of the civil war in Rwanda instigated by an RPF incursion from Uganda into Rwanda in 1990 that culminated in the 1994 genocide. The chapter critically explores: the detailed, reliable and relevant information that was available to the British Government in the period 1990–94 regarding the RPF and the violent conflict in Rwanda and the RPF; Britain's role in the UNSC regarding Rwanda; British Government ministers' responses to oral and written questions within the House of Commons; and the views of elite respondents to this study regarding political will and genocide in Rwanda. This chapter demonstrates that the British Secret Intelligence Service (SIS) deployed an intelligence network in the Great Lakes region of Africa; throughout the 1990s, SIS maintained a relationship with senior commanders of the RPF, who themselves maintained a strong intelligence network in Rwanda. This ensured a wealth of relevant intelligence was available to the British Government about the conflict in Rwanda throughout the early 1990s.

Chapter 7 reveals the British Government's justifications for its response to genocide in Rwanda, including its reluctance to define the atrocities in Rwanda as 'genocide'. The chapter concludes by summarising the positive steps undertaken by the United Kingdom to negate its legal responsibility in terms of the UNGC, establishes that its objective was incompatible with its legal obligation, and hence infers a degree of complicity in genocide by omission.

Chapter 8 is the concluding chapter of the book and discusses the scope of liability of states and other elite bystanders as responsible actors, and the nature of complicity of elite bystanders to genocide, as well as the equally important ongoing relationship between powerful political institutions and international law. The chapter also details Britain's relationship with the post-genocide Government of Rwanda, despite the latter's responsibility for two decades of volatility and gross violations of human rights in Rwanda and the Democratic Republic of Conqo (DRC). It is only by piecing together all aspects of the tragedy and instability in the Great Lakes region of Africa throughout the past 20 years that criminologists and international jurists will have a more realistic understanding of how international law might intervene to prevent a genocide like that which occurred in Rwanda from ocurring in the future.

Chapter 2

Global Elite Bystanders, Genocide Complicity and International Law

> Complicity assumes great importance for protecting individuals, peoples and weaker States.
>
> (Quigley 1986: 130)

Chambliss's 1989 Presidential address to the American Society of Criminology, on state-organised crime, demonstrated how states can be crucial in the organisation and support of activities that violate their own laws and international laws, and in so doing, fulfil their own broader political and economic objectives. This chapter explores international criminal law and complicity as a lens for understanding the scope of liability for states as responsible actors in an era when certain states have substantially greater resources than others, and when those more powerful states seek to influence events abroad.

The actions and motivations of perpetrators, victims and bystanders has long been the focus of Holocaust and genocide studies, with the greatest emphasis given to the perpetrators of genocide and the least studied group being that of the bystander (Ehrenreich and Cole 2005; Goldhagen 1996; Browning 1993). In criminological scholarship generally, the role of bystanders, and the degree to which the bystander can be held accountable for their actions and inactions, has been under-analysed (Cohen 2001; Kroslak 2003). In criminological terms, there is no detailed definition of the term 'bystander', nor any effort to understand the role of bystanders in violations of international criminal law. Such an exploration must include the actions and inactions of the global ruling elites and states who form organised groups with enforceable and non-enforceable legal obligations to society as a whole, and who are physically distanced from the *loci* of criminality as opposed to the individual bystander *in situ*.

Dominant understandings of the individual bystander

Historically, academics have described 'bystanders' as individuals sited at the very location of an 'event' or 'atrocity' (see Hilberg 1992; Beres 1989;

Ehrenreich and Cole 2005), as opposed to non-individuals such as corporations, states, organisations or communities, which are sited external to the locus being researched. Cohen correctly argues that the term 'bystander' has acquired the pejorative meaning of 'passivity and indifference' (2001: 140). Definitions and delimitations of the 'bystander' label are complex, with the term being utilised historically in a number of contradictory ways, typically and erroneously implying absolute non-participation. On occasion, the label of bystander has been applied to non-rescuers who did nothing out of the ordinary during the Second World War either to help other people or resist the Nazis. Hilberg argues that the bystanders of the Second World War were those who 'looked away, asked no questions, and refrained from talk in public' (1992: 195). Antipodally, Adolf Eichmann's plea to being a bystander during his trial in 1961 highlighted the historical abuse of the term. Todorov's definition of the bystander includes an element of responsibility, as 'passive spectators who are responsible at most for not coming to the aid of those in danger' (Todorov 1996: 231). Although Todorov does not define the limits of the label, the definition certainly infers that bystanders have a responsibility towards the victims of genocide, albeit a moral obligation. Valier (2005) deals solely with the predicament of individuals and ordinary members of the public who, through no fault of their own, find themselves bystanders at the scene of a crime.

Common to philosophical understandings is the portrayal of the bystander as a non-participant spectator. Problematic to such a universally accepted definition of the bystander is that it fails to recognise that an individual's mere presence at the scene of a crime could be perceived as a form of participation, allowing potentiality for the bystander to mutate into a perpetrator. Also problematic is that such philosophical definitions dictate that a bystander must necessarily be present at the actual *locus* of the crime.

Current understandings of the institutional bystander

In sharp contrast to the individualistic bystander scholarship of philosophers, Stohl alludes to the 'international system of states' as bystanders, but disappointingly provides no further clarification of whom he includes in his 'system' or what their responsibilities may include as external actors in genocide (1987: 151). Refreshingly however, Stohl does define bystanders as 'observers outside the threatened area' (ibid) thereby negating the requirement for a bystander to be necessarily present at the actual locus of an event. Similarly, Kroslak discusses the bystander not as an individual but 'as an organized group … who find themselves *outside* a genocidal society' [author's own emphasis] (2003: 161). However, Kroslak also accepts the pejorative meaning of the bystander, namely the passivity and indifference of the bystander. This is a surprising stance from Kroslak in her study of the French Government as a collective external bystander in the case of the genocide in Rwanda. The

French were in fact neither passive nor indifferent in their position as 'an organized group' external to the Rwandan genocide.

As the twentieth century has shown, the international community and whole governments are frequently bystanders to genocidal events and the inaction of these global elites is essential to those who carry out crimes against humanity and genocide. Yet with the exception of Stohl (1987), Cohen (2001) and Kroslak (2003), there is a dearth of literature that explores the concept of governmental actors a as bystanders with recognised legal duties and obligations in relation to international law.

Any proposed definition of the bystander that fails to envelop not only the individual bystander present at the *locus* of an ongoing crime or atrocity, but also the global elite bystanders situated external to an international crime or atrocity, is seriously flawed. Furthermore, for a definition to be useful it must also acknowledge that the bystander is not obligated to act on merely moral grounds. In the case of genocide, global elite bystanders who are external to the *loci* of atrocities and who are signatories to the relevant United Nations Conventions and Treaties, are under strict legal and political obligations to act so as to prevent or halt atrocities such as that of genocide. Should the global elite bystander fail to fulfil such obligations, there is a potential for such actors to be redefined as perpetrators, thereby obfuscating the apparent clarity of what Cohen has described as an 'atrocity triangle' (2001: 14) and the assertions of those who solely define bystanders as entirely separate entities to either victims or perpetrators (Ehrenreich and Cole 2005; Barnett 1999; Hilberg 1992). Cohen's 'atrocity triangle' maintains that bystanders, perpetrators and victims occupy three quite separate points on a triangle, which opens up a paradox in the formal separation of roles. Cohen utilises Bosnia as an example to infer that external international actors who protect genocidal regimes 'are definable as bystander states' (2001: 18). This suggests that although legally culpable, they are definable as a bystander as opposed to a perpetrator, which is something of a contradiction and so rather confusing. This conundrum suggests the need for a degree of fluidity between points of the atrocity triangle, permitting transitions between the identifiers of bystander, perpetrator and victim as appropriate.

Power as a prerequisite of the institutional bystander

Power can be seen as a group's ability to attain a desired goal with or without the consent of those affected, and it is this argument that informs Ehrenreich's and Cole's (2005) Perpetrator–Victim–Bystander model. This model determines that bystanders to genocide are powerless and lack the required authority, legitimacy or control that would enable them to undertake any action other than to show support for, or avoidance of, the perpetrators of genocide. Here I argue strongly that it is these very characteristics – power, authority, legitimacy and control – that underpin the decision-making processes of governments, states, corporations, communities and transnational organizations (e.g. the UNSC) all of which can be usefully included in this book's concept of global elite bystanders. Such actors do possess power, authority, legitimacy and control, and are part of an institutional decision-making process, with privileged access to knowledge of global conflict and clear indicators of imminent or ongoing genocide from such sources as diplomatic and military intelligence reports, human rights agencies, international media broadcasts and publications, etc. In the case of external governments which are signatories to the appropriate convention, they *do* have the legitimacy to lead, *are* in a position to influence a majority of the international community and *are* in control of the regulation of resources necessary to intervene either to pre-empt or to prevent the genocidal process.

By insisting that the bystander role is powerless, Ehrenreich and Cole have negated any potential to utilise or develop their model for this study of British Government as a global elite bystander. Power is of the utmost importance to this study since power is a pre-requisite of any global elite bystander in achieving their desired goal, irrespective of the impact of that goal on those affected by the atrocity. This power allows the global elite bystander to have an impact on the genocidal process by: (a) supporting the perpetrator group; (b) defeating the perpetrator group or sufficiently reducing its power, authority, legitimacy and control that the genocidal process comes to an end; or (c) using its power to prevent their elite collectivity from taking action, which in itself has an impact on the genocide. Passivity and inaction by a global elite bystander is especially important in the early stages, when warning signs can be clearly detected. Should such bystanders refuse to take early preventive steps, then in the words of Cohen (2001: 162), 'perpetrator governments can go safely ahead, relying on their allies, patrons and donors to hold back'. As such, one can conclude that if the bystander state does not utilise its power to intervene, the perpetrator state becomes empowered. There is therefore a correlation of power between bystander and perpetrator states, and this correlation will be apparent this book's discussion of London's role during the 1994 genocide in Rwanda.

But how does international law construct the responsibility of the global elite bystander in general, and in relation to genocide in particular?

International law – 'no police force or bailiffs ...'

> 'Law', in common parlance, means a rule which (unlike a rule of ethics) is actually capable of enforcement through institutions created for that purpose. But 'law' in the phrase 'international law' does not automatically have this quality: it has no police force or bailiffs, and its courts lack the capacity to punish for contempt or for disobedience to their orders.
>
> (Robertson 2002: 85)

Although international law as a framework of social control has existed for centuries, it is only in the past few decades that it has evolved into an established legal framework for the control of individual and institutional state actions. The meaning of the phrase 'international criminal law' depends on its use. There are a wealth of definitions, not all of which are consistent. However, most legal scholars currently agree that a recognisable body of international criminal law does exist although the precise parameters of this body of law are often unclear, perhaps due to the rapid and complex developments of our global society. In its widest context, the source of international criminal law is derived from the general principles of international law recognised by civilised nations and therefore found in the customary law accepted by states, the general criminal law recognised by nations, and the treaties which govern particular conduct. The Military Tribunal at Nuremberg defined an international crime as 'such act universally recognized as criminal, which is considered a grave matter of international concern and for some valid reason cannot be left within the exclusive jurisdiction of the State that would have control over it under ordinary circumstances' (cited in Kittichaisaree 2001: 3).

Crimes of the state

Crimes of the state are arguably the most serious of all crimes, and yet international jurisprudence relating to the concept of state criminality is relatively sparse. In the pre-First World War era, international law failed to confront the Turkish *Ittihad* Government's destruction of one million Armenians. Neither did it address the acts of the German high command that commissioned the building of the Berlin–Baghdad railway and were witnesses to the Ottoman Empire's genocidal policy towards the Armenian labour. Indeed, the German state and German corporations were themselves complicit in their use of Armenian forced labour (see Dadrian 2007) but were not confronted under international law. In respect of the Armenian tragedy, it appears that the law proved incapable of disentangling crimes of genocide from criminal aspects of colonialism, national development and international trade, and from prosecuting them.

The concept of state responsibility for international crimes emerged in its current incarnation in the shadow of the First World War, when human rights law was developed as a cluster of legal norms focused principally on protecting the individual against crimes committed by the state. These legal norms imposed obligations upon states to ensure rights for individuals and, because these obligations were contracted on an international level, they were capable of breaching the impenetrable wall of state sovereignty. Such a concept of state responsibility for international crimes was however relegated into the background after the Second World War, the horrors of which provoked a significant expansion and codification of international criminal law through the development of *individual* criminal responsibility under international law (Jorgensen 2000; Kramer and Michalowski 2005).

Recent developments have demonstrated a legislative shift towards the recognition of state criminal responsibility, however. The concept of states being responsible for breaches of international criminal law was formally adopted in Part I of the UN International Law Commission (ILC) Draft Articles on Responsibility of States for Internationally Wrongful Acts received by the UN General Assembly in 2001 (ILC 2001b), which is perhaps one of the most important topics that the ILC has addressed. The ILC decided in 1976 to include an article in its Draft Articles on State Responsibility, which makes a distinction between international crimes and international delicts within the context of internationally unlawful acts (ILC 1976: 95–112). Of significance is the distinction drawn in Article 19 of the ILC Draft Articles 1976 between international crimes and international delicts within the context of internationally unlawful acts. It provides 'an internationally wrongful act resulting from the breach by a state of an international obligation so essential for the protection of fundamental interests of the international community that its breach was recognised as a crime by that community as a whole, constitutes an international crime' (Kittichaisaree 2001: 7). All other internationally wrongful acts were termed international delicts.

Article 37 of the ILC Draft Articles 2001 provides that a state responsible for a wrongful act is obliged to give satisfaction for the injury thereby caused, in so far as it cannot be made good by restitution or compensation (ILC 2001a: 263). Shaw clarifies that 'satisfaction may consist of an acknowledgement of the breach, an expression of regret, a formal apology or another appropriate modality' (2003: 720). Examples of such international crimes ensconced by said articles were, amongst others, aggression, the establishment or maintenance by force of colonial domination and genocide.

The ILC Articles are quite explicit in stipulating that wrongful acts of persons in ostensible authority may be attributed also to the states they serve. Under Article 8, acts committed by individuals 'shall be considered an act of State under international law, if the person or group of persons is in fact acting on the instructions of, or under the direction or control of that state, in carrying out the conduct' (ILC 2001b). Article 9 adds that 'the conduct of a person, or group of persons, shall be considered an act of State under international law if the person, or group of persons, is in fact exercising elements of governmental authority in the absence or default of the official authorities, and in circumstances such as to call for the exercise of those elements of authority' (ibid). The Draft Articles thus make quite clear that the acts of empowered individuals can be directly attributable to the state that empowered them. One area of increasing sophistication is the act of complicity in the law of state responsibility. Complicity liability arises where a state facilitates the commission by another state of an internationally wrongful act. The principles of international law as formulated by the ILC have dictated that complicity in the commission of a crime against peace, a war crime or a crime against humanity, is a crime under international law (ILC 1957: 374–8). Therefore a concept of state complicity has been developed in international jurisprudence to enable the prosecution of those who knowingly assist, aid, abet, procure or counsel genocide but without ever actually wielding the machine guns or machetes.

However, the question as to whether states can be criminally responsible continues to be highly controversial (see Jorgensen 2000). Some have argued that the concept is of no legal value and cannot be justified in principle, not least because of the problem of exacting penal sanctions from states (Brownlie 1963: 150–4).

This book argues that in the concept of state responsibility, human rights and criminological concerns can be merged in a meaningful way through a literal use of the concept of state crime being applied to activities which are unambiguously in breach of international law. Genocide undoubtedly presents one of the most complete and glaring illustrations of the violation of international law and the laws of humanity; there is no crime in the twentieth century that has been more costly, more devastating, and more global in its impact than genocide.[1]

International law and genocide

Central to any discussion of international law applying to state crime is the UNGC, which was adopted by the United Nations on 9 December 1948, and entering into force on 12 January 1951.[2] The UNGC is an international treaty which draws on elements of international criminal law, international humanitarian law, and international human rights law (Schabas 2000: x). As the International Court of Justice (ICJ) noted in its 1951 advisory opinion, 'the principles underlying the Convention are principles which are recognized by civilized nations as binding on States, even without any conventional obligation'.[3] The ICJ has therefore recognized the UNGC's proscription against the crime of genocide as a part of customary international law and a *jus cogens* norm.[4] It is worth noting that the UNGC's definition of genocide has been echoed in subsequent legal mechanisms without significant amendment, including the statute creating the International Criminal Tribunal for the Former Yugoslavia (ICTY), the statute creating the International Criminal Tribunal for Rwanda (ICTR) and the Rome Statute for the creation of the International Criminal Court (Jorgensen 2000). In his analysis of the UNGC, Robertson explains:

> At its highest, namely when the State takes life pursuant to a policy of genocide, this right is so forcefully protected by international law ... that it justifies armed intervention by other states whether pursuant to

> Chapter VII or by way of a unilateral humanitarian mission, and the International Court of Justice may order 'provisional measures' against a government under the Genocide Convention
>
> (2002: 102)

The jurisdiction of the UNGC also extends, in Article III, to include conspiracy to commit genocide, and complicity in genocide as crimes under international law. The Statutes of both the ICTY and the ICTR likewise contain two notable provisions on responsibility for genocide: 'complicity' in genocide and 'aiding and abetting genocide'. The prosecutor of the ICTY argues that 'any assistance, even as little as being involved in the operation of one of the camps [militia training camps]' constitutes sufficient participation to meet the terms of complicity (Schabas 2000: 294). It must be acknowledged that negligence is incompatible with the specific intent requirement of genocide; as the ICTR observed in the Akayesu case (1996),[5] an individual cannot be guilty as a participant in genocide 'where he did not act knowingly, and even where he should have had such knowledge' (ibid: 227). Schabas describes complicity in genocide as those who 'aid, abet, counsel and procure or otherwise participate in criminal offences' (ibid: 285) and has interpreted the proceedings of the ICTR in the Akayesu case as 'aiding means giving assistance to someone', while 'abetting involves facilitating the commission of an act by being sympathetic thereto' (ibid: 292–3).

Complicity in genocide: direct state responsibility

Within the UNGC, there is an affirmation that states may not fail to act in the face of mass atrocities directed at the destruction of a particular group. But no state has ever been held accountable for such a contravention under the terms of the UNGC, despite the weight of evidence available, for example, of the knowing abandonment of prisoners in the Nazi death camps by Allied troops during the Second World War (see Hilberg 1992; Breitman 1998). As previously noted, the ICTR has successfully secured several convictions on charges of complicity in genocide (details of all judgements are available at http://www.ictr.org). However, those have been convictions of individuals. Fitzmaurice argues that this could be due to the 'considerable difficulty in expressing [the] idea in the text of the Convention of the direct responsibility of a state for genocide or for any of the other acts enumerated in Article III, which includes complicity in genocide' (cited in Jorgensen 2000: 277).

The subject of states' direct responsibility for genocide, in addition to their responsibility for the failure to prevent or punish acts of genocide, was debated during the conceptualisation phase of the UNGC, when the United Kingdom proposed an amendment to Article V. The amendment stated that '[c]riminal responsibility for any act of genocide as specified in Articles II and IV shall extend not only to all private persons or associations, but also to States, governments, or organs or authorities of the State or government, by whom such acts are committed' (Jorgensen 2000: 36). The proposed amendment was however rejected and the ambiguous wording of Article IX continues to be the subject of much close examination and debate (Schabas 2000; Jorgensen 2000). Interestingly the ICJ's interpretation of Article IX does not exclude any form of state responsibility. Nor was the responsibility of a state for acts of its organs excluded by Article IV, which contemplates the commission of an act of genocide by 'rulers' or 'public officials' (Jorgensen 2000: 269).

One can conclude therefore that rules for states are often codified in international law, as is the case with the UNGC. However, the role of norms should not be underestimated in providing guidelines for the action of states when confronted with atrocity. All international treaties are established under the rubric of the United Nations ostensibly to achieve 'peace', and therefore the United Nations's mission is always constructed as a humanitarian one.

The purposes of the United Nations as per Chapter I(1) of the UN Charter is to maintain international peace and security and '[i]n order to ensure prompt and effective action by the United Nations, its Members confer on the Security Council primary responsibility' for same (UN 1945).[6] The UNSC is empowered under the Chapter VII provisions of the Charter to 'determine the existence of any threat to the peace, breach of the peace, or act of aggression' and to take military and nonmilitary action to 'restore international peace and security' (ibid).[7] The United Nations, after approval by the UNSC, traditionally sends peacekeepers to regions where armed conflict has recently ceased or paused, to enforce the terms of peace agreements and to discourage combatants from resuming hostilities. Since the United Nations does not maintain its own military, peacekeeping forces are voluntarily provided by its Member States.[8]

Humanitarian intervention under scrutiny

> There is at least a tension, if not an outright contradiction, between the rules of world order laid down in the Charter and the rights articulated in the Universal Declaration. ... The Charter bans force violating state sovereignty; the Universal Declaration guarantees the rights of individuals against oppressive states. ... The issue of humanitarian intervention arises from this tension.
>
> (Chomsky 1999: 73)

The circumstances that allow the use of force under the rubric of humanitarian intervention in international society have come under considerable scrutiny. Many academic discussions focus on the question of whether there is a legal right of humanitarian intervention.[9] While some academics perceive the principle of contemporary humanitarian interventions as an emerging norm predicated on the foundation and realisation of human rights, others feel that its inconsistent use would suggest otherwise (Zolo 2002). Pivotal to this debate is the alleged tension between humanism and neo-humanitarianism,[10] the latter of which is 'distinguished by the explicit manipulation of humanitarianism for political or military gain on the ground in a conflict or as a substitute for political and military action' (Mills 2005: 162). In his celebrated April 1999 Chicago speech, ex-Prime Minister Blair outlined his 'doctrine of the international community', in which he justified wars over Kosovo, Afghanistan and Iraq by reference to humanitarian motives, rather than military interests (1999). Scholars and policy-makers are struggling to balance these two seemingly conflicting sets of norms in international society.

These conflicting sets of norms create a paradox. For its first 45 years, the United Nations was firmly associated with the principle of non-intervention in the internal affairs of sovereign states, a fact that helped to explain the support that it received from governments of post-colonial states. Then, in the post-Cold War era, the United Nations progressively became associated with a pattern of interventionism, often on at least partly humanitarian grounds. From being an institution for the non-use of force, the United Nations has become an instrument for the use of force (see Mingst and Karns 2000, 2007). As Noam Chomsky points out, this conflict is embodied in the two main pillars of international law and international order: the UN Charter and the Universal Declaration of Human Rights (1999: 73).

The evolving practices of humanitarian intervention in the 1990s

Heated debate over humanitarian intervention is compounded by the scale of the issue: in the last decade of the twentieth century, it is estimated that globally 35 million people faced humanitarian crises. As the International Commission on Intervention and State Sovereignty (ICISS) states, in this 'revolutionary decade for humanitarian action … the Security Council authorized more than a dozen Chapter VII operations in response to conscience-shocking human catastrophes' in territories ranging from northern Iraq to East Timor (ICISS 2001b: 220). Such a response from the UNSC signaled a notable sea change: during the Cold War, not one resolution mentioned humanitarian intervention (Weiss 2004: 38). Gowan argues that this sea change has now become the official principle of the European Union and 'the mobilizing doctrine of Western military intervention around the world from the Middle East to the Balkans, from sub-Saharan Africa to the Caribbean' (2001: 150). It was the NATO bombing of Yugoslavia in support of ethnic Albanian Kosovars in the spring of 1999 that brought to the fore the Western claim of universal positive obligation for the protection of global human rights (Zolo 2002: 84). Claims that such an intervention being launched on the basis of positive obligation for the universal protection of human rights would be unlawful were countered by the former UN Secretary-General Kofi Annan who proclaimed in September 1999:

> If humanitarian intervention is, indeed, an unacceptable assault on sovereignty, how should we respond to a Rwanda, to a Srebrenica – to gross and systematic violations of human rights that affect every precept of our common humanity?
>
> (Annan 2000: 48)

Humanitarian intervention and the prevention of genocide

Most states in the international community have accepted, through their ratification of the UNGC, an obligation 'to prevent and to punish' such acts. Therefore, genocide has been placed beyond the protection of the domestic jurisdiction clause of the UN Charter Article 2(7) and must be viewed as an international crime. Kuperman is solidly of the opinion that there is overwhelming political support for a positive obligation on states to intervene to prevent genocide (2001: 1). The authors of the UNGC created an obligation to repress genocide, and legal analysis affirms that intervention in respect of genocide may include military action. However, in terms of the UNGC this was viewed as a right rather than as an obligation (Schabas 2000: 498).

During the 1990s, the UNSC determined that a number of domestic humanitarian and human rights crises, including genocide, constituted 'threats to international peace and security'. In doing so, the UNSC went beyond the traditional concept of threats, though not in a manner that contradicted the 1948 UN Charter. This determination by the United Nations reinforced the need for the international community to prevent and punish genocide, and provided states with Chapter VII powers to impose mandatory sanctions or authorise the use of military force against a genocidal regime. Military action by states for the purposes of preventing genocide had now become an obligation as opposed to a right. Schabas is of the opinion that the permanent members of the UNSC who were extremely reluctant to use the word 'genocide' in a resolution concerning the Rwandan crisis, acted as such for fear that it 'would impose an obligation to act to prevent the crime' (ibid: 495). International law offers little support though for states acting individually in response to acts of genocide, with Article VIII of the UNGC stating that only multilateral responses are legitimate.

One may therefore argue that a neo-humanitarian norm supporting humanitarian intervention in instances of genocide has developed in international society over the course of the 1990s, a norm which empowers states with legislative provisions that positively oblige them to prevent humanitarian crises. In essence, this norm asserts that, when all other diplomatic actions have failed, states have the responsibility to employ military force against another state in order to protect civilians in danger. The report of the ICISS concludes: 'Sovereign states have a responsibility to protect their own citizens from avoidable catastrophe … but when they are unwilling or unable to do so, that responsibility must be borne by the broader community of states' (2001a). It is therefore arguable that the failure of states to fulfil their positive obligation to prevent genocide, thereby protecting 'threats to international peace and security', is a breach of international law.

Conclusion

This chapter has highlighted the legal standing in relation to complicity in genocide and other violations of international criminal law and provides a useful lens for understanding the scope of liability of states and other global elite bystanders as responsible actors in genocide, albeit not the primary perpetrators or co-authors. As noted by Quigley, 'complicity assumes great importance for protecting individuals, peoples and weaker States' (1986: 130).

In summary, global elite bystanders to genocide, as described in this chapter, are liable to charges of complicity in genocide if they fail to undertake their positive obligations, such as the prevention and suppression of acts of genocide or any of the other acts enumerated in Article III, where a clearly missed moment of opportunity to act has been identified and where reliable intelligence clearly warned of imminent and serious humanitarian risks. Determining such charges necessarily requires determination of the consequences to the crime of genocide when global elite bystanders do not comply with such treaty obligations.

Genocide complicity by global elite bystanders may also be inferred if their actions are shown to have assisted, aided or abetted the perpetrators of genocide in some form. Article III of the UNGC makes punishable four forms of participation in the crime: conspiracy, direct and public incitement, attempt and complicity. Again, this necessarily requires determination of the consequences to the genocide induced by such complicit bystanders. It must be proven that the global elite bystander had knowledge of the genocidal intent of the principal perpetrators albeit without necessarily sharing that genocidal intent. Knowledge can therefore be the *mens rea* of complicity in genocide.

These two points of international law relating to 'bystander' complicity in genocide, as opposed to direct involvement in genocide are of key significance to this book and may have been committed by global elite bystanders to the Rwandan genocide of 1994. Later chapters of this book will undertake a rigorous analysis of data gathered to establish whether the global elite bystanders of the British Government failed to undertake their positive legal obligations in terms of the UNGC in 1994. We will also examine whether they could be deemed to be complicit in terms of international law in the genocide of 1994, either by crimes of omission or commission. This analysis will enhance our current understandings of the motivations behind the role of such actors in genocide and further develop the concepts of state crime and of global elite bystander complicity in genocide.

Chapter 3

Reading the Histories of Rwanda

The politicisation of history is a helpful tool to mask political manipulation by internal and external powers during systematic massacres of innocent civilians, and this was the case in Rwanda. It is therefore essential to establish some essentials regarding the ancient relationships between the Hutu and Tutsi, and the impact of the socially constructed racist categories of its European colonisers, to establish whether it is appropriate for the Rwandan genocide to be viewed within the continuation of the logic of colonialism. Obviously there is no linear relationship between the historical past and the complex present of Rwanda; several strands of history are pivotal to one's understanding of the Rwandan genocide. The violence needs to be placed within the broad contexts of pre-colonial Rwanda; the German and Belgian colonisation of Rwanda, France's role in Rwanda post-independence and Britain's relationship with the Rwandan diaspora in Uganda. Rwanda has a long and complex history, and the development of ethnic identities and ethnic conflict is only one of the many issues that are evident in the country's rich historiography. It is therefore of interest to explore whether racialisation was introduced in the colonial era, or whether it was already evident in the pre-colonial period.

Deconstructing the racialisation of social categories, colonisation and genocide in Rwanda

> We need to interpret interpretations more than to interpret things
>
> (Montaigne, cited in Derrida 2001: 351)

Contradictory mythical versions of pre-colonial histories of Rwanda have been developed over the years by Tutsi and Hutu participants alike, and '[b]oth allude to distant dark deeds reeking of blood and turn truth into an open-ended concept' (Prunier 1995: 357). The first King of Rwanda, Gihanga, was the son of a deity known as the Root of Man, and early historians place his rule around the tenth century. However, contemporary historians doubt that he or his celebrated descendents ever actually existed. The term 'Banyaruanda/Banyarwanda' refers to the one tribal people found in Ruanda,[1] all of whom are speakers of the Kinyarwandan language. Despite being one tribal people, the Banyaruanda were divided into three social groups, namely the Twa (0.5 per cent), Hutu (87 per cent) and Tutsi (12.5 per cent). Although unsubstantiated, the popular thesis holds that in Rwanda's pre-colonial past these three groupings arrived during different historical periods. The Twa were allegedly the first to arrive, followed by the Hutu agriculturalists,[2] and lastly the Tutsi pastoralists,[3] who arrived in successive waves from about the fifteenth century onwards (Sirven et al. 1975: 56–7). Up until 1860, historians knew very little about how the terms 'Twa', 'Hutu' and 'Tutsi' were used in social discourse. It was simply unclear whether these terms denoted social or physical classifications, for instance, and there was little agreement on how to describe those differentiated by the terms – races, castes, ethnicities, tribes or simply groups.

The situation is much clearer from 1860 onwards, and substantive research reveals that it was the mid-eighteenth-century King Rwabugiri of the Tutsi royal court in Rwanda, who either began or reinforced a process of ethnic polarisation between Hutu and Tutsi, which led to the oppression of the peasant classes, but most particularly the Hutu peasantry. Rwabugiri introduced a number of practices, most notably ubuhake cattle clientship and a labour pre-station called uburetwa, both of which came to denote the loss of local political autonomy (Mamdani 2001). Put simplistically, ubuhake was an unequal clientship contract entered into by two men, a patron and a client. Under *ubuhake*, a Tutsi patron would give his Hutu client a cow, which would hopefully reproduce, and future calves would be shared between the patron and client. Prunier (1998: 14) suggests that the clients in such obligations 'would never get anywhere at all with this deal'. Uburetwa, the despised corveée labour service through which populations regained access to the lands they had lost to Rwabugiri, was central to these practices and applied only to the Hutu. The labour due under uburetwa was set at one day out of five (Lemarchand 1970: 122). Tutsi commoners, while also heavily exploited by the ruling central court and its aristocracy (Newbury 1978: 21, 1988: 12; Vidal 1969: 399; Chrétien, 1985: 150), enjoyed freedom from uburetwa; their labour service consisted merely of seasonal maintenance work to the grounds of the aristocracies' enclosures (Newbury 1988: 140).

The literature of early European explorations into central Africa suggests that the first European to visit the Ruanda area was John Hanning Speke, an explorer and officer of the British Army, in 1858. Speke was obsessed with race, and developed several hazardous hypotheses on the origins of the Tutsi. When Speke arrived in what was then the Kingdom of Ruanda, he decided that the Tutsi, being of lighter skin and more European in appearance than the Hutu people they ruled, must be a superior race and not native to Ruanda. Speke concluded they must be descendants of the biblical figure Ham, one of the sons of Noah. Such Hamitic concepts have since been widely discredited and are now referred to as the 'Hamitic Myth' (see Sanders 1969 and Biddis 1966 for detailed discussion).

During an 1898–99 traverse through Ruanda, a young Cambridge student observed the 'obvious hatred in which they (the Hutu) hold their over-lords (the Tutsi), [but] there seems to be no friction' (Grogan 1902: 130). He also noted the 'far-famed unity and power of the Ruanda people' and the 'the pervading air of prosperity ... a striking indication of the possibilities of native races left to work out their own destiny' (ibid: 121). Although noting distinct physical differences between the social categories of Hutu and 'their absolute antithesis' in the Tutsi (ibid: 129), Grogan found that they shared other traits, describing all social categories collectively as 'the terrible people of Ruanda, whose reputation has spread far and wide' (ibid: 126). Grogan boldly maintains that 'of all the liars in Africa, I believe the people of Ruanda are by far the most thorough' (ibid: 142). In 1876, an Arab informed Stanley on a visit to Karagwe in Tanzania, that the people of Ruanda were 'a great people, but covetous, malignant, treacherous, and utterly untrustworthy' (1878: 455).

The writings of other early European visitors show a remarkable consensus about the individual demeanour of Hutu and Tutsi as well as their conduct towards one another. Of the Tutsi of Ruanda, Frederick wrote, 'one received the impression of being in the presence of an entirely different class of men, who had nothing further in common with the "niggers" than their dark complexion' (1910: 54), whilst Meyer noted that 'lying [by Tutsi] is not only customary with strangers but a permanent and deeply rooted defect ... the Tutsi consider themselves as the top of creation, from the standpoint of intelligence and political genius' (1916: 15). By contrast, Meyer observed the Hutu to be a singularly servile, boisterous and cowardly people, whose sense of dignity and self-esteem had been dulled almost to extinction by centuries of bondage to their Tutsi masters. Of the Hutu in Urundi, Meyer wrote: 'Due to four centuries of terroristic rule, they have become slaves in thinking and acting, though not so slave-like in character as the Banyarwanda under their Hamitic despots [Tutsi overlords]' (ibid: 15).

There is little evidence for such conclusions. However, this racial characterisation does appear to reflect empirical observations of the political dominance by the group referred to as the 'Tutsi'. Beyond this empiricism, those sweeping generalisations were most likely made on the basis of anecdotal interaction with very small numbers of locals, and then probably mostly Tutsi aristocracy. A further hindrance to any rigorous analysis of the populations encountered by the colonisers was the language barrier, with Philipps recording that 'in this era, no English–Kinyaruanda interpreter, black or white' was in existence (1923: 234).

Reductionist versions of Rwandan pre-colonial history

David and Catharine Newbury have for nearly four decades been at the forefront of scholarship in Rwanda's pre-colonial past and have contributed much to the development of pre-twentieth century historical knowledge. So too has the unpublished PhD dissertation of Alison Des Forges, 'Defeat Is The Only Bad News', which is the subject of a conference paper and chapter by David Newbury (2011).

Despite such distinguished scholarship being available, there are journalists and academics with discernible sympathies towards the current Rwandan Tutsi-dominated government of Paul Kagame who remain naively dogmatic in their portrayal of a pre-colonial Rwandan history where people lived side by side harmoniously, free from political hierarchies. After the genocide, 'the RPF secured the support of sympathetic journalists and aid workers uninformed about the region … and without research experience in Rwanda' (Pottier 2002: 109). These sympathetic outsiders include Linda Melvern, who portrays 'political correctness RPF-style' (ibid: 75); Philip Gourevitch, who is keen 'to toe the RPF-functional line and thus reproduce the view that all Hutu refugees are genocidal extremists who collectively deserved their fate in eastern Zaire' (ibid: 57); and Fergal Keane, who reproduces 'the RPF's reductionist version of how Hutu–Tutsi–Twa relations had evolved' (ibid: 65). Such support from outsiders undoubtedly lends an air of authenticity to the RPF Government of Rwanda's skewed version of history. In an attempt to establish that the introduction of the static categories of Hutu and Tutsi, and the violent divisionism of the same, was the sole doing of the colonisers, post-genocide mythical versions of pre-colonial history have suggested that nineteenth-century Banyaruanda had categories that were fluid to the extent that one could readily change their identity from that of a Hutu to a Tutsi merely, for example, by the acquisition of more head of cattle. Reductionist versions also dismiss the biological evidence of 'average genotype and phenotype differences affecting blood groups, sickle cells, and lactose digestion' between Hutu and Tutsi (Mann 2005: 432). Keane and Melvern's simplistic and Kagame-style politically correct version of pre- and post-colonial history, respectively, as background to the genocide, dismisses the body of post-independence scholarship available, producing instead a mythical historical account that is easily digested by readers who are unfamiliar with the complex history of the Great Lakes region. One can only speculate whether these accounts are the result of lack of research experience and knowledge of the region, or solely a desire to adhere to Kagame's party line.

Such oversimplifications by academics and journalists alike, and the consistency with which they ignore or misrepresent post-independence scholarship on Rwanda is staggering. Keane, in common with many other contemporary commentators, obscures the complex and fundamental developments that emerged in the country in the second half of the nineteenth century, developments that, as previously noted, saw the loss of Hutu peasantry land rights as a result of unjust intervention by the conquering Tutsi royal court, which also exerted oppressive control over labour. Such a distortion of pre-colonial history negates any responsibility of the mid-nineteenth-century

Tutsi aristocracy in the ensuing division between the country's social groups, placing all responsibility on the shoulders of the colonisers. It is essential to acknowledge that there were critical changes to racialisation in Rwanda during the colonial period, but scholarship clearly evidences that Rwanda had a foundation for racialisation prior to the arrival of any European into the country.

Racialised political development in Rwanda by Europeans – The Hamitic myth

Colonisation arrived later in Rwanda than in many other African countries, probably due to its isolated inland location, which lacked resources of benefit to the dawning industrialisation that heralded the great European powers' staking of effective claims to the interior of the African continent. At the Berlin Conference of 1884–85,[4] Germany gained the rights to Ruanda-Urundi, although it was not until 1894 that Count von Goetzen made the first German expedition through Ruanda and encountered a cordial welcome from the Tutsi Mwami, the supreme ruler of the land, who, as previously noted, held an overwhelming concentration of power. Such a warm welcome was a disappointment to the German army, which was armed for battle. The Germans informed the Mwami that they now controlled East Africa, including Ruanda, and history indicates that the Mwami was willing to recognise the German protectorate. Lemarchand asserts that such willingness of the court to co-operate with the Germans was due to the perceptiveness of the ruling Tutsi in realising the potential reciprocal benefits of such an arrangement, as 'the terms of the quid pro quo made it possible for the crown to expand its hegemony far beyond the limits of its original jurisdiction' (Lemarchand 1970: 57). Newbury (1988) has carried out a detailed academic analysis of the intertwining roots of Rwanda's history and has convincingly explained how often, without the acquiescence of colonial officials, Tutsi leaders took advantage of European weaponry and administrative structures to intensify the power they had previously developed in their late-nineteenth-century state formation. Des Forges (cited in Newbury 2011: xxx) notes that the Rwandan Court were able to manipulate the Germans with 'a combination of courtesy and deception'. Consequently, as Tutsi power intensified, their control over resources increased and their access to Western education, colonial positions and other desirable statuses became monopolised, further excluding the ever more subordinated Hutu.

Germany ruled the one administrative territory of Ruanda-Urundi until 1916, when it lost the First World War and was forced to forfeit its colonial possessions. At the resulting Paris Peace Conference of 1919, which was organised to negotiate the dispersal of German colonial possessions, the British fully intended to take all of German East Africa, including Ruanda-Urundi. Indeed, the British claimed and received a majority share. However, the Milner–Orts agreement of 30 May 1919, dictated that Belgium be granted Ruanda-Urundi, despite London's desire to acquire these fertile high lands (Louis 2006: 221). Orts placated the British by advising them that the region was 'not worth the anger of England' (Louis 1963: 256). Britain acquired a part of Ruanda, however, namely the Kigezi District of north-western Ruanda, which despite being ethnologically as well as geographically part of the native pre-colonial Kingdom of Ruanda, became absorbed by the British Government as part of its Ugandan protectorate – to this day it is part of the south-western corner of Uganda. The British mandate oversaw the destruction of immemorial and natural boundaries, with the Banyaruanda of south Kigezi district being pulled in a different political direction from their neighbours. Evidence of this early-twentieth-century partition of the Kingdom of Ruanda into 'Belgian Ruanda' and 'British Ruanda' is found in the scholarship of geologists rather than historians. In his exploration of the geology of the Lake Albert Rift Valley, Wayland (1921: 346) repeatedly refers to the the Kigezi District as 'British Ruanda'. Philipps also describes a 'British portion of Ruanda [that] lies politically within the Kigezi District', in his study of the Birunga volcanoes of Kigezi-Ruanda-Kivu (1923: 233).

Belgium was already ruling the neighbouring Congo, and ruthlessly exploiting its vast natural wealth, when it was assigned Ruanda. While Belgium ruled the Congo directly, Ruanda was assigned as a 'trust territory', which dictated that its rule was subject to supervision from the League of Nations and later, the United Nations. Neither institution provided much input, and the Belgians were at liberty to govern their new acquisition largely as they wished.

Belgian reform of the colonial state of Rwanda

The Belgians arriving in their new territory of Rwanda were familiar with the racist hypotheses regarding the origins of the social categories of Hutu, Tutsi and Twa that had been articulated by nineteenth-century explorers. Such erroneous hypotheses led to deeply ingrained views and attitudes by the Belgians regarding the Rwandese social groups they were dealing with, and were to later govern the decisions made by the Belgian colonial authorities, which impacted greatly on the natives themselves. The Tutsi were perceived to have Caucasian features and thus were interpreted by the colonisers as a naturally superior people to the less-evolved Hutus, and this conferred on them ideological, political and economic status. Being exemplary colonial administrators, the Belgians undertook an exhaustive census in 1933 using physical characteristics to determine who was a Hutu and who was a Tutsi. On the basis of this system of classification, the entire population were issued with an identity card that fixed once and for all their societal position as Hutu, Tutsi or Twa. This 'scientific' classification and its political institutionalisation had a profound effect on Rwandan culture and produced an indelible 'reality' of Tutsi superiority and Hutu inferiority. Tutsi citizens were elevated to positions of power and sent to missionary schools for education at the expense of the Hutu citizen's literacy requirements. Belgian administrators replaced Hutu chiefs with Tutsi. The replacement policy was so extensive that by 1959, 43 out of 45 chiefs and 549 of 559 sub-chiefs were Tutsi (Destexhe 1995: 40). In addition '83 per cent of posts in such areas as the judiciary, agriculture and veterinary services were held by Tutsi' (Kamukama 1997: 21). Such discriminatory practices served to intensify Hutu bitterness and resentment towards the Belgians and their Tutsi clients and enhanced ethnic polarisation between the Hutu and Tutsi.

It was almost a quarter of a century after the arrival of the Belgians that nationalist intellectuals called on their fellow Hutu in 1957 to rise up against the political monopoly of the Tutsi in a published text known as the 'Bahutu Manifesto' (Nkundabagenzi 1961: 20–9). The text alluded to the humiliation and socio-economic inferiority suffered by the Hutu community and promoted the central idea that Rwanda was a Hutu country and should be ruled by Hutu (Prunier 1995: 45).

When decolonisation came to Rwanda in 1959, it arrived in the form of a Hutu revolt, aided by the outgoing resident Belgian colonisers who turned against the ruling Tutsi whom they had supported since colonisation. Hutu militancy was encouraged and as a result of the violent Hutu revolution, about 10,000 Tutsi were driven out of the country into exile in Uganda (Newbury 1988: chs 9, 10). Lemarchand argues that 'from the moment the residency decided to throw its weight on the side of the Hutu as happened in late 1959, the die had been cast; short of a miracle, the period of Tutsi rule was bound to come to an end' (1970: 485). To formalise this radical change in power structure in Rwanda, the Belgians, against the wishes of the United Nations Trusteeship Council, called for local elections in June 1960 in which the main Tutsi political party refused to participate. The Belgians dismissed protestations and went ahead with the election that saw the Parmehutu (Parti du movement de l'émancipation des Bahutu), a political party identifying exclusively with Hutus, easily winning the first elections in 1960 and 1961 and, with them, control of Rwanda's political process. In September 1961, some 80 per cent of Rwandans voted to end the Tutsi monarchy, thus confirming the proclamation of a republic the previous January by the Parmehutu-led government. These events became known as the 'Hutu Revolution' (Des Forges 1999). Formal independence was granted on 1 July 1962 with the radical Hutu Grégoire Kayibanda becoming Rwanda's first president. The Hutu Revolution caused great angst amongst the Tutsi elites in Burundi who were determined not to cede power when independence came, thus stimulating ethnic violence in post-independence Burundi (see Lemarchand 1995: 76–105). The outgoing Belgian colonisers had fewer resources than the French or British, and no valuable minerals to protect in Rwanda; when pressured, they simply abandoned the country, with little thought for post-colonial institutions (Mann 2005: 433).

Around this period a process of 'dual' historical development began to emerge, namely the visible history unfolding within Rwanda, and the less visible aspects of history unfolding outside its borders, the key protagonists of the latter being the Tutsi diaspora in exile in Uganda.

The visible post-independence Rwandan history

There were two major political trends that dominated post-independence Rwanda. First, the principles of the Hutu Revolution of 1959 guided official policy, which meant that Hutus dominated the government and military, often to the exclusion of Tutsis.[5] Grégoire Kayibanda ruled from 1962 to 1973, and was more than willing to use ethnic terror and sow division in order to maintain rule. Kayibanda presided over a series of anti-Tutsi massacres in the early 1960s and 1970s, with ethnic violence becoming a central feature of Rwanda's politics (Prunier 1995: 54–61). Despite maintaining strong limits on Tutsi advancement through a system of regional and ethnic quotas, Rwanda's second president Juvénal Habyarimana, who ruled from 1973 to 1994, was more moderate than his predecessor.[6]

The second trend was regionalism, which shaped significant political conflict among the Hutus. Kayibanda came from Gitarama prefecture in the south-central region of the country and his rule largely benefitted Hutus from his home region. Habyarimana, by contrast, came from Gisenyi prefecture, and his rule largely benefitted northerners, in particular those from the north-west. By 1990, Hutus from the north-west held a near-total monopoly on key posts in the Government, the Army and in parastatal companies (Reyntjens 1994). The political situation in Burundi also shaped Rwandan politics, with repression by Tutsi in Burundi radicalising Hutu in Rwanda. During the 1960s and 1970s, both countries became locked into severe ethnic discrimination, backed by policed repression and punctuated by bursts of pressured emigration (Hintjens 1999: 279). There is little evidence, however, of physical violence against the Tutsi between 1979 and 1990 in Rwanda.

The less visible post-independence Rwandan history

During the 30-year period following Rwanda's independence, the scattered Tutsi diaspora led to the emergence of communities of 'Rwandans abroad', causing division between the Tutsi remaining in Rwanda who accepted the restrictions imposed on them by the Hutu regime, and those Tutsi in exile who were angered by their loss of status in their home country (Interviews Rwanda, 2005). The politically motivated violence of 1959 had started the flow of refugees and discrimination and violence perpetuated the flow. Those fleeing included many ex-soldiers, and they now formed the core of Tutsi military ambitions to one day return to Rwanda as an invading force. Their initial efforts at invasion failed miserably and led to successive waves of retaliatory violence against Tutsi in Rwanda. By the late 1970s, almost half a million Tutsi had fled the country, with over 80,000 seeking refuge in Uganda; there they suffered systematic discrimination under the repressive regime of president Milton Obote, faring only slightly better under Idi Amin. Following Amin's expulsion, Obote returned to power in December 1980 in what was widely recognised as a fraudulent election. One of Obote's defeated opponents in the election, Yoweri Museveni, soon began to prepare for a continuation of the struggle for power in Uganda, but this time by arms. In 1981 Museveni launched his National Resistance Army (NRA) and among his small band of dissidents were two Rwandan exiles, one of whom was Paul Kagame, who had become a follower of Museveni in the late 1970s, joining his small resistance organization formed in 1978 in Tanzania to help overthrow Idi Amin. Kagame became a specialist in intelligence matters, rising to the head of military intelligence in Museveni's army following Milton Obote's overthrow in 1986. By the time Kampala was captured on 26 January 1986, Museveni had a force of 14,000 fighters, 500 of whom were Rwandan. However, deep-seated resentment towards the Tutsi refugees in Uganda remained (Waugh 2004). An interview with a member of the clergy illustrates the root cause of the disdain felt towards the Tutsi militia:

> These Rwandese use the most unacceptable counter-insurgency strategies; they herd women, children and old-people into houses and set the houses on fire; they rape women in the presence of their male relatives, and at times, they force the male relatives to sleep with those women after they [the soldiers] have exhausted their sexual desire … These people are determined to spread slim [HIV] to Acholi. I also witnessed them mutilate unarmed people including school children.
>
> (Otunnu 2000: 32)

With the armed struggle over in Uganda, Museveni sent Kagame and other officers of the NRA overseas as part of a nation-building programme and to develop their military skills. Kagame was aware that guerrilla movements rarely succeed without at least tacit support from a friendly regime in a nearby country; he correctly reasoned that, having helped Museveni take power in Uganda, Museveni would in turn support Kagame's own pro-active movement dedicated to overturning the regime in Kigali and establishing a very different type of government in the homeland of the Tutsi refugees.

The Rwandan Alliance for National Unity (RANU), formed in 1980 in Uganda, was an explicitly militant formation whose ambition was the right of Rwandan refugees to return home. After Museveni's successful bush war ended in 1986, RANU turned to Tito Rutemara, an academic and RANU member held in high esteem, and charged him with developing a new and more military strategy for their cause:

> Throughout the 1960s and 1970s, there was this vague thought that we wanted to return to our homeland, but there was no strategy. There were no leaders ... Fighting to go back was going to be the only way. There would be no negotiating with the dictatorship. We decided we would have to fight the dictatorship.
>
> (Interview with Rutemara, Rwanda, 2005)

In June of 1987, Rutemara opened a clandestine school in Uganda teaching theoretical strategies to his 'cadres'. In December 1987, RANU adopted what it viewed as a more appropriate name, the Rwandan Patriotic Front (RPF), with constitutional declarations akin to those of the NRA and with 'chapters' being organised across Africa, Europe and North America (ibid). The RPF was led by Paul Kagame who, in his capacity as Uganda's head of military intelligence from November 1989 until June 1990, had received training in military tactics and intelligence methods at the US Army's Fort Leavenworth Command and General Staff College in Kansas. Museveni also sent Kagame to Britain, North Korea and Canada for military training (Ottunu 2000: 33).

Conclusion

There are various ways in which cultures can construct ideologies of racialisation. Such ideologies can be, and are, attached to any number of characteristics that serve to socially transform a collection of individuals within a culture into a group – gender, nationality, age, sexual preference, social and economic class, religion and much else, including race. Attributing fixed 'differences' to particular groups is clearly a tool of power in which certain people are defined as 'other', and usually as inferior. Interestingly, the converse is true of Rwanda where it was the minority Tutsi who were constructed by the European colonisers as 'other' or 'alien', albeit superior to the majority/inferior Hutu, identifying the Tutsi as having originated from the northern hemisphere and being both distinct and superior to the 'Negroid' populations of Sub-Saharan Africa.

As previously noted, an analysis of the body of literature relevant to the racialisation of social categories throughout Rwandan history indicates that pre-colonial wars in Ruanda were either against foreign tribes or were internal affairs between lineages fighting for power. A credible and substantive body of literature also exists to establish that Banyaruanda relationships were by no means harmonious. This literature contradicts the position adopted and promoted by the current Rwandan regime, which encourages academic and journalistic 'sympathetic outsiders' to embrace and spread an idyllic perspective on pre-colonial society and history. Such histories discount three decades of rigorous post-independence scholarship on Rwanda, and lend authenticity and legitimisation in the outside world to a palimpsest with ideological underpinnings.

Pre-colonial Rwanda encountered discriminatory practices by the ruling Tutsi monarchy against the differing social categories that were the Banyaruanda, although racialisation of social categories in Rwanda was undoubtedly accentuated by the arrival of the Europeans who failed to acknowledge that 'roots can be very tangled things' (Memmi 1991: 31), with mixed Hutu/Tutsi or Hutu/Twa backgrounds and intermarriages being ignored. The racial distinctions created by the European colonisers for the purpose of the old colonial policy of *divide et impera* thereafter exacerbated and racialised existing inequalities. What had been oppressive conditions in pre-colonial Rwanda became a more cohesive policy as a result of colonisation.

The supposedly foreign Hamitic origins of the Tutsi, once used to defend their inherent right to rule, were used to justify plans by the majority Hutu group to drive the minority Tutsi group out of Rwanda. As such, the Rwanda genocide must be viewed within the logic of colonialism and racialism of the colonised. Racialism in the context of colonisation is a frequently recurring theme in documented instances of genocide and mass violence. There were elements of racism in the genocide of the Herero, where the norm was for white settlers to refer to black Africans as 'baboons' and to treat them accordingly (Bridgman and Worley 2004: 20). By utilising racialisation as a lens to understand the pre-colonial and colonial experiences of the Banyaruanda, this chapter has illuminated the specificities of racism encountered, revealing insights into when and how race became a salient signifier of difference in Rwanda. This necessarily included the development of what is known as the Hamitic myth, which evidences how the hegemonic power of racist dogma, perpetrated for political reasons and in the interests of European imperialist designs, profoundly affected the colonial history of Rwanda.

Europeans did not invent the categories of Hutu and Tutsi. Neither would it be acceptable to infer that this was a peaceful, harmonious culture pre-colonisation. The Banyaruanda's exposure to protracted European racialisation did, however, have a long-term and cumulative effect, which resulted in repeated violence; as such it has played a significant role in what is now referred to as the Rwandan genocide of 1994, and any valid analysis of the genocide of 1994 and its aftermath should be viewed within the continuation of the logic of colonialism and indeed neo-colonialism.

Chapter 4

The Spectre of Genocide in Rwanda, and Its Aftermath: Internal and External Responsibility for Genocide

Critical to our understanding of the role of the British Government in the Rwandan genocide are the complex events of several years immediately before the genocide, from 1990 until early 1994. In the early 1990s, these axes of Rwandan political history collided when, in October 1990, the Tutsi exiles under the banner of the RPF invaded Rwanda from southern Uganda. Despite official denials at that time, these moves *did* receive the tacit support of Ugandan President Yoweri Museveni, who viewed the RPF favourably in light of its extensive help in the early 1980s, when Museveni was himself battling to win Uganda's own civil war. Ugandan support for the RPF was not explicit, however, as Museveni worried that Uganda may lose foreign aid if it was seen to be sponsoring a foreign invasion.

The formation of the RPF and its objectives were supported throughout by Britain, which appeared to be priming the RPF to take power in Rwanda. By 1988 it was an open secret in Uganda and Rwanda that Tutsi members of the Ugandan Army were planning an invasion of Rwanda (Kuperman 2004). Destexhe has evidenced that military training for the guerrilla RPF in Uganda was provided by British forces at its military base in Jinja, Uganda (1995).

By August 1990, the RPF was in the final stages of preparing a full-scale invasion of Rwanda, despite the GOR undertaking several significant political steps in an effort to avert the invasion; this included facilitating the repatriation of Tutsi refugees from Uganda as demanded by the RPF, with the initial phase scheduled for November 1990. As such, Uganda–Rwanda negotiations on the rights of refugees to claim Rwandan nationality had reached 'an advanced stage' (Mamdani 2001: 159) when the RPF attacked in October 1990. Only three days prior to the attack, Habyarimana had announced key concessions to refugees at the UN General Assembly in New York (ibid). However, the RPF chose not to allow the validity of Habyarimana's initiatives to be tested. It is ironic that the incursion should happen during a rare period of internal reform as opposed to repression in Rwanda, and during a period when President Habyarimana was making every effort to appease the rebel force.

Many African analysts believe that the order for the October 1990 invasion could not have been given without the knowledge, approval and active assistance of the Pentagon's Central Intelligence Agency (CIA) and Britain's SIS. Both agencies were heavily engaged in Uganda at this time (Madsen 1999). Such assertions are corroborated by written submissions to the ICTR (Chossudovsky 2005).

This RPF incursion into Rwanda on 1 October 1990 instigated three years of civil conflict in Rwanda between the Hutu-dominated GOR and the Tutsi-dominated guerrilla rebels of the RPF, and this conflict culminated in the genocide of 1994.

Pressure for political change in Rwanda

The violent civil war in Rwanda came at a time of major political change. Like most other African states, Rwanda was a single-party state for almost the entire post-colonial period. However, the end of the Cold War changed the political status quo on the continent. With the fall of communism in Europe, some Western donor countries and many African elites no longer accepted single-party dictatorships, and so it was in Rwanda. In 1991, under pressure from France, which was then Rwanda's principal international backer, President Habyarimana formally ended the exclusive rule of his party, the *Mouvement Révolutionnaire National Pour le Développement* (MRND). Immediately thereafter, a vigorous, largely Hutu opposition quickly arose to challenge the president and his party. The Hutu opposition was strongest in the southern, south-western and south-central regions. The largest opposition party was the *Mouvement Démocratique Républicain* (MDR) (Lemarchand 1970; Bertrand 2000; Prunier 2002: 121–6).

One cannot fully understand the manoeuvring of the Habyarimana regime against both its internal challengers and the omnipresent threat from the RPF without also fully understanding first, the role of France in its military and ideological support of the Francophone GOR, and second, the French view towards Francophone Africa in general. This is discussed in some details in Chapter 6. For the purposes of the current chapter, it will suffice to say that a prolonged civil war between the RPF and the GOR commenced as a direct result of the RPF invasion of October 1990. It is arguable that the civil war was sustained for such a lengthy period of time due primarily to the fact that both sides received substantial Western assistance, the RPF from the United States and United Kingdom; the GOR from France and its francophone allies. This has led to suggestions that the conflict in Rwandan was in fact a proxy war between Western powers (Prunier 2009).

The Arusha Peace Accords

The period following an agreement on ending internal conflict can often be even bloodier and more dangerous than the period before the agreement.

> The Arusha Peace Accords, which ostensibly ended the ongoing conflict in Rwanda between an exiled Tutsi guerrilla group (the RPF) and the Hutu Government of President Juvénal Habyarimana, are a tragic example of a negotiated agreement failing miserably in its implementation.
>
> (Stettenheim 2000: 213)

As previously alluded to, the power of the Rwandan ruling elite led by President Habyarimana was being challenged by both the Tutsi-led RPF guerrillas and the GOR's Hutu political opponents. As a direct result, the ruling elite's singular grip on power began to disintegrate. The ruling elite, known as *akazu*,[1] had profited under Habyarimana, and most had little intention of relinquishing their power without a fight. The campaign of the Rwandan ruling elite included: explicit linkage of the Tutsi-dominated RPF guerrilla army resident in Uganda, to the resident Tutsi population living in Rwanda (Prunier 2002: 138); significant expansion of the FAR and launching of a civilian defence programme;[2] and development and training of a youth militia in 1992 and 1993. Indeed, by early 1994, there appear to have been at least several thousand militiamen in different parts of Rwanda (Des Forges 1999: 101) belonging to one of two organisations associated with political parties. These militia were known as the *Interahamwe*[3] and the *Impuzamugambi*.[4] The hardliners also developed lists of RPF supporters and leading moderate Hutu opponents in Kigali, which some scholars have labelled 'death lists': during the first days of the April 1994 massacres, hardliners systematically assassinated these leading Hutu opposition figures and RPF supporters (Destexhe 1995). These developments clearly indicate that the hardliners pursued irregular tactics to keep power and were prepared to use lethal violence against civilians if need be (Prunier 1995: 222, n22; Gasana 2002: 243). Hardliners formed the private *Radio et Télévision Libres des Milles-Collines* (RTLM) radio station in mid-1993, broadcasting highly inflammatory content. Repeated articles in the *Kangura*[5] stressed that Hutus and Tutsis were different 'races', and made nativist Hutu claims against the 'Hamitic' Tutsi, thereby presenting the armed conflict as a race war (Chrétien 1995: 95–9, 110–11).

As Hutu hardliners developed irregular and radical tactics, so too did RPF leaders clandestinely prepare for combat 'using their international connections to procure the material they needed' (Waugh 2004: 61). Recruitment processes escalated and the RPF, which had numbered only 4,000 men when it made its first incursion into Rwanda in October 1990, had an estimated strength of 20,000 by the end of 1992. 'Despite the outward show of diplomacy and commitment to peace negotiations [by the RPF], the internal reality was one of preparations for war' (ibid).

In April 1992, under domestic and international pressure, President Habyarimana formed a coalition government with the political opposition, which in turn began peace negotiations with the unenthusiastic RPF rebels.

Conflict continued in Rwanda until, after numerous rounds of negotiations, the two sides reached a power sharing agreement, which was signed on 4 August 1993. Since the peace talks had been held in Arusha, Tanzania, the agreement became known as the Arusha Accords.[6] According to McQueen, the Arusha Peace Agreement was arguably 'a significant victory for the RPF' (2005: 99) and laid the groundwork for a 'virtual political revolution in Rwanda' (Adelman and Suhrke 1996: 25). Politically, the agreement called for a broad-based transitional government (BBTG) with a specified exact composition and this formation was to be followed by multiparty elections (McQueen 2005: 99–100).

Under the terms of the Arusha Peace Agreement, the RPF was permitted to station a number of its diplomats, including Tito Rutemara, in the national parliament building in Kigali ironically referred to as the *Conseil National de Dévеloppement* (CND), and the RPF was permitted to protect these diplomats with a battalion of 600 soldiers (Interview, Rutemara, Rwanda, 2005). According to several reports, the rebel leadership continually breached the peace agreement by stealthily shipping hardware and other military supplies to troops within the CND building. The RPF also maintained a network of cells around the country (Des Forges 1999: 180–1) and, according to at least one former RPF officer, who has since broken ranks, the RPF leadership sought to destabilise the Habyarimana regime through political assassinations, the killing of civilians (Ruzibiza 2005), and the laying of landmines (Dallaire 2004: 156). Gribbin (2005) provides a detailed analysis of the RPF's skills, concluding that the RPF domination at the bargaining table in fact accelerated the forces of Hutu extremism.

There was one other key component of the Arusha Accords. They called for a ceasefire and featured a major role for the United Nations in implementing the Accords with the deployment of an international peacekeeping force to monitor the ceasefire and to secure Rwanda during its period of transition.

Establishment of UNAMIR

Both signatories to the Arusha Accords consented to the establishment of a neutral international peacekeeping force in Rwanda under the responsibility and command of the United Nations. Despite their reluctance, the UNSC acquiesced to provide a peacekeeping mission in Rwanda to monitor the proper implementation of the Arusha Peace Agreement. McQueen argues that the UNSC's reluctance to manage the peace process with any degree of commitment or determination foreshadowed its later response to the genocide (2005: 101). One UNSC member explained such reluctance as being largely due to the Council's 'collective misunderstanding of the Arusha peace negotiation process', having only become engaged in the process after the signing of the Arusha Accords:

> When the Arusha talks concluded in August 1993 with a recommendation for a UN peacekeeping operation, there was anxiety in some parts of the Council that the peace process had effectively boxed in the United Nations and predetermined a key issue, which was not the prerogative of the negotiators. The parties had drafted provisions in the peace agreement with implications for UN action. These were predicated on the Council saying yes to the adoption of a resolution for a peacekeeping operation. This situation caused a sense of irritation with Rwanda on the part of some Council members, including the British member, which may well have played a part in conditioning subsequent responses in 1994.
>
> (Interview, 2006)

The mandate ultimately agreed upon by the Security Council in Resolution 872 of 5 October 1993 was considerably reduced in scope from that suggested as being appropriate by the Accords. Resolution 872 established a United Nations Chapter VI[7] peacekeeping mission to Rwanda, which was designated as the United Nations Assistance Mission for Rwanda (UNAMIR) with an initial six-month mandate, subject to review and renewal in April 1994.[8] The main objective of UNAMIR was to assist in the monitoring of the peace process and the maintenance of security without proactive use of force in Rwanda during the period of transition. The UN mission was also required to monitor a weapons-secure area to be established by the Rwandese parties in and around Kigali and the observance of the ceasefire agreement. However, the agreed allocation 2,538 troops to UNAMIR was actually below the numbers considered to be an absolute minimum by the Canadian Force Commander, General Roméo Dallaire (Interview, London, 2005). Dallaire stated that he was frustrated in his efforts from the outset because mobility provision for UNAMIR was seriously lacking, as a result of the United Nations having no self-owned logistical reserves on which to depend, and the majority of troop-contributing nations also failed to provide the requested materials (ibid). According to one member of the UNSC, 'UNAMIR was given a more robust mandate than was normal, but the force structure given to the UNAMIR Force Commander – in particular the equipment and readiness levels of the force – bore no relationship to what was really needed' (Interview, New York, 2006).

As an aside, Burundi shares the same ethnic makeup as Rwanda, but in Burundi it was the Tutsis that controlled the state after independence (Lemarchand 1970). As part of Africa's wave of democratisation, Burundi ended one-party rule and in June 1993 voters elected the country's first Hutu president, Melchior Ndadaye. A few months later, Tutsi military leaders assassinated Ndadaye, causing reverberations in Rwandan political circles. A campaign of intense Tutsi-led repression followed, which resulted in the death of approximately 50,000 Hutu and Tutsi in Burundi, and led to about 900,000 Hutu refugees fleeing into Rwanda (World Bank 1994: 12–13).

The Hutu ruling elite in Rwanda, often referred to as the 'hardliners', seized on these events to corroborate their claims that the Tutsis of Rwanda would never share power and sought only the domination of Hutus (Prunier 1995, 2002), causing panic within the majority of the Hutu population of Rwanda (Gasana 2002: 226). It was the ruling elite and domestic Hutu opposition's responses to such threats posed by Tutsi military challenges that would have huge consequences for Rwanda in 1994 (Hintjens 1999: 259).

It is accepted that there were clear indicators throughout the 1990s, and in particular soon after the deployment of UNAMIR in Rwanda in October 1993, that all was not well within the country. In 1992, the Belgian Ambassador had warned his government that Hutu Power advocates were 'planning the extermination of the Tutsi of Rwanda' and in April 1993, the UN Special Rapporteur on Summary, Arbitrary, and Extrajudicial Executions said that massacres of Tutsis already constituted genocide (Stanton 2005: 271–3).

Planning a genocide?

Throughout the early 1990s, there was growing evidence of the importation of arms into the country and reports that weapons were being distributed to civilians (see McNulty 2000). Indeed, intelligence regarding the location of arms caches within the country was made available to the UN Secretariat at least as early as 11 January 1994, when General Dallaire sent a version of the now infamous 'genocide fax' to New York. That a fax was sent on the 11 January 1994 by Dallaire is undisputed; what is questionable is the actual content of the fax and whether this communication raised concerns for the safety of the Belgian contingent of UNAMIR and/or alluded to the planned genocide of the Tutsi of Rwanda, as is now alleged. The prosecution at the ICTR attempted to prove that genocide of the Tutsi was planned ahead of April 1994 by Hutu extremists. However, there is a distinct lack of documentary evidence of any Rwandan government plan to commit genocide – no orders, minutes of meetings, notes, cables, faxes, etc. – and as such the key piece of evidence for the prosecution was the production of a copy of the 'genocide fax', the single document upon which claims of a planned genocide depended. This fax, which was produced in the ICTR, was allegedly sent by General Dallaire, stationed in Kigali, to General Baril of the Department of Peace Keeping Operations (DPKO) in New York on the night of 10–11 January 1994, and alludes to the claims of a UN informant in Rwanda who advised Dallaire that the ruling government party planned to exterminate Tutsis and was training civilians for that purpose, and also that there was a plan to kill Belgian soldiers to provoke the withdrawal of UN forces. However, the fax did not make its first public appearance until 28 November 1995 when it was placed in the UN files in New York and subsequently 'leaked' to a journalist in Belgium and the British *Observer* newspaper (Philpot 2004). A UNAMIR commission created in early November 1995 had been tasked with analysing all UNAMIR cables, faxes and reports in an effort to collate all information that was suggestive of a pre-planned genocide of Tutsi; however, in its report dated 20 November 1995, no such evidence was found, and there was no trace of the 'genocide fax' (ibid).

The copy of the 'genocide fax', dated 11 January 1994 and produced by the prosecution as an exhibit in the ICTR Military II trial in October 2005, was proven by the defence counsel to have been altered and did not correspond with the copy of the 'genocide fax' held in the UN archives in New York. The archived 'genocide fax' document, which was placed in the UN files on 28 November 1995, is marked, 'This cable was not found in DPKO files. The present copy was placed in the files on November 28th, 1995.' It is signed by Lamin J. Sise, a UN official. The document contains other handwritten notes made on it after its receipt that day. The copy fax produced by the prosecution of the ICTR had the name and fax number of the sender, Sise's note, and other notes removed.

It was ultimately disallowed and instead 'entered into the record the copy of the fax contained in the DPKO files bearing the name of the British Army source' (Black 2005). This 'British Army source' refers to a Colonel R. M. Connaughton, based at Camberley, Surrey, England, the home of the Sandhurst British Military Academy, as well as several other British Army establishments. Colonel Connaughton sent the fax to New York in November 1995, and his name and fax number appear at the top of the UN archived document. There was however no cover letter forwarded with the fax explaining who sent it, why it was sent, nor is there anything indicating why this document was accepted by the United Nations in New York and placed in the DPKO files. Other commentators have noted further discrepancies in the archives of the ICTR (Barouski 2008), whilst the testimonies of General Dallaire have been contradictory on occasion and highlight, by his own admission, his many breaches of UN protocol, communicating directly with the DPKO rather than through his UNAMIR superior, Jacques-Roger Booh-Booh (Black 2005).

Although the exact content of the fax that was forwarded by Dallaire to the UN DPKO cannot be established, responses to it from the DPKO suggest that the conditions for UNAMIR in Rwanda were more difficult than the UNSC had first thought. Interviews with former ambassadors of the UNSC confirm that this significant contribution to the knowledge of escalating violence within Rwanda was never revealed to the Security Council, although it is suspected that the information would have been shared privately with the French and US Ambassadors (Interviews, London, 2005/06). Sir Edward Clay, the roving ambassador with responsibility for Rwanda before and during the genocide, confirmed that, despite meeting personally with Dallaire in March 1994, he was not made aware of the fax of 11 January 1994, nor of security risks to Belgian peacekeepers. With regards to the 'genocide fax', Clay states, 'It's one of these things that with the benefit of hindsight should have been given more attention, but it wasn't' (Interview,

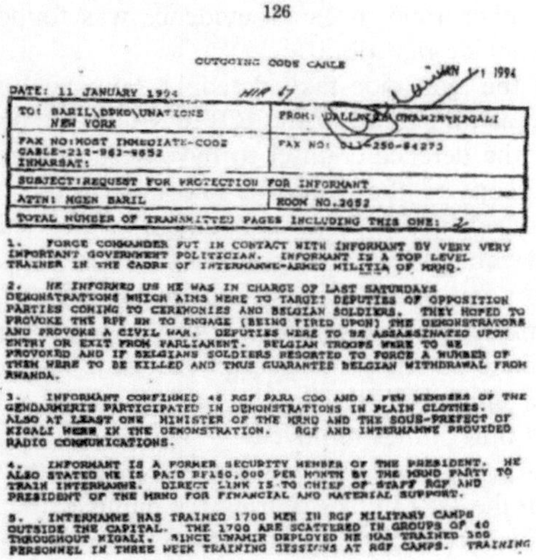

126

OUTGOING CODE CABLE

JAN 11 1994

DATE: 11 JANUARY 1994

TO: BARIL\DPKO\UNATIONS NEW YORK	FROM: DALLA[illegible]UNAMIR\KIGALI
FAX NO: MOST IMMEDIATE-CODE CABLE-212-963-9852 INMARSAT:	FAX NO: [illegible]-250-84273
SUBJECT: REQUEST FOR PROTECTION FOR INFORMANT	
ATTN: MGEN BARIL	ROOM NO. 2052
TOTAL NUMBER OF TRANSMITTED PAGES INCLUDING THIS ONE: 2	

1. FORCE COMMANDER PUT IN CONTACT WITH INFORMANT BY VERY VERY IMPORTANT GOVERNMENT POLITICIAN. INFORMANT IS A TOP LEVEL TRAINER IN THE CADRE OF INTERHAMWE-ARMED MILITIA OF MRND.

2. HE INFORMED US HE WAS IN CHARGE OF LAST SATURDAYS DEMONSTRATIONS WHICH AIMS WERE TO TARGET DEPUTIES OF OPPOSITION PARTIES COMING TO CEREMONIES AND BELGIAN SOLDIERS. THEY HOPED TO PROVOKE THE RPF BN TO ENGAGE (BEING FIRED UPON) THE DEMONSTRATORS AND PROVOKE A CIVIL WAR. DEPUTIES WERE TO BE ASSASSINATED UPON ENTRY OR EXIT FROM PARLIAMENT. BELGIAN TROOPS WERE TO BE PROVOKED AND IF BELGIANS SOLDIERS RESORTED TO FORCE A NUMBER OF THEM WERE TO BE KILLED AND THUS GUARANTEE BELGIAN WITHDRAWAL FROM RWANDA.

3. INFORMANT CONFIRMED 48 RGF PARA CDO AND A FEW MEMBERS OF THE GENDARMERIE PARTICIPATED IN DEMONSTRATIONS IN PLAIN CLOTHES. ALSO AT LEAST ONE MINISTER OF THE MRND AND THE SOUS-PREFECT OF KIGALI WERE IN THE DEMONSTRATION. RGF AND INTERHAMWE PROVIDED RADIO COMMUNICATIONS.

4. INFORMANT IS A FORMER SECURITY MEMBER OF THE PRESIDENT. HE ALSO STATED HE IS PAID RF150,000 PER MONTH BY THE MRND PARTY TO TRAIN INTERHAMWE. DIRECT LINK IS TO CHIEF OF STAFF RGF AND PRESIDENT OF THE MRND FOR FINANCIAL AND MATERIAL SUPPORT.

5. INTERHAMWE HAS TRAINED 1700 MEN IN RGF MILITARY CAMPS OUTSIDE THE CAPITAL. THE 1700 ARE SCATTERED IN GROUPS OF 40 THROUGHOUT KIGALI. SINCE UNAMIR DEPLOYED HE HAS TRAINED 300 PERSONNEL IN THREE WEEK TRAINING SESSIONS AT RGF CAMPS. TRAINING

Figure 4.1

London, 2006). However, it is now evident that the 'genocide fax' was in fact a fabrication.

Renewal of UNAMIR mandate, April 1994

Evidence that the political process had stalled and was being undermined by President Habyarimana and his ruling Hutu elite caused concern in the UNSC when the members discussed the renewal of UNAMIR's mandate in January, and again in the first week of April 1994. The decision to authorise a continued UN presence was disputed and 'several of the larger financial contributors, with the notable exception of France, seemed determined to shut down UNAMIR unless the peace process was put back on track quickly' (Interview, New York, 2006). Supporters of the peacekeeping force, on the

127

2/2

FOCUS WAS DISCIPLINE, WEAPONS, EXPLOSIVES, CLOSE COMBAT AND TACTICS.

6. PRINCIPAL AIM OF INTERHAMWE IN THE PAST WAS TO PROTECT KIGALI FROM RPF. SINCE UNAMIR MANDATE HE HAS BEEN ORDERED TO REGISTER ALL TUTSI IN KIGALI. HE SUSPECTS IT IS FOR THEIR EXTERMINATION. EXAMPLE HE GAVE WAS THAT IN 20 MINUTES HIS PERSONNEL COULD KILL UP TO 1000 TUTSIS.

7. INFORMANT STATES HE DISAGREES WITH ANTI-TUTSI EXTERMINATION. HE SUPPORTS OPPOSITION TO RPF BUT CANNOT SUPPORT KILLING OF INNOCENT PERSONS. HE ALSO STATED THAT HE BELIEVES THE PRESIDENT DOES NOT HAVE FULL CONTROL OVER ALL ELEMENTS OF HIS OLD PARTY\FACTION.

8. INFORMANT IS PREPARED TO PROVIDE LOCATION OF MAJOR WEAPONS CACHE WITH AT LEAST 135 WEAPONS. HE ALREADY HAS DISTRIBUTED 110 WEAPONS INCLUDING 35 WITH AMMUNITION AND CAN GIVE US DETAILS OF THEIR LOCATION. TYPE OF WEAPONS ARE G3 AND AK47 PROVIDED BY RGF. HE WAS READY TO GO TO THE ARMS CACHE TONIGHT-IF WE GAVE HIM THE FOLLOWING GUARANTEE. HE REQUESTS THAT HE AND HIS FAMILY (HIS WIFE AND FOUR CHILDREN) BE PLACED UNDER OUR PROTECTION.

9. IT IS OUR INTENTION TO TAKE ACTION WITHIN THE NEXT 36 HOURS WITH A POSSIBLE H HR OF WEDNESDAY AT DAWN (LOCAL). INFORMANT STATES THAT HOSTILITIES MAY COMMENCE AGAIN IF POLITICAL DEADLOCK ENDS. VIOLENCE COULD TAKE PLACE DAY OF THE CEREMONIES OR THE DAY AFTER. THEREFORE WEDNESDAY WILL GIVE GREATEST CHANCE OF SUCCESS AND ALSO BE MOST TIMELY TO PROVIDE SIGNIFICANT INPUT TO ON-GOING POLITICAL NEGOTIATIONS.

10. IT IS RECOMMENDED THE INFORMANT BE GRANTED PROTECTION AND EVACUATED OUT OF RWANDA. THIS HQ DOES NOT HAVE PREVIOUS UN EXPERIENCE IN SUCH MATTERS AND URGENTLY REQUESTS GUIDANCE. NO CONTACT HAS AS YET BEEN MADE TO ANY EMBASSY IN ORDER TO INQUIRE IF THEY ARE PREPARED TO PROTECT HIM FOR A PERIOD OF TIME BY GRANTING DIPLOMATIC IMMUNITY IN THEIR EMBASSY IN KIGALI BEFORE MOVING HIM AND HIS FAMILY OUT OF THE COUNTRY.

11. FORCE COMMANDER WILL BE MEETING WITH THE VERY VERY IMPORTANT POLITICAL PERSON TOMORROW MORNING IN ORDER TO ENSURE THAT THIS INDIVIDUAL IS CONSCIOUS OF ALL PARAMETERS OF HIS INVOLVEMENT. FORCE COMMANDER DOES HAVE CERTAIN RESERVATIONS ON THE SUDDENNESS OF THE CHANGE OF HEART OF THE INFORMANT TO COME CLEAN WITH THIS INFORMATION. RECCE OF ARMED CACHE AND DETAILED PLANNING OF RAID TO GO ON LATE TOMORROW. POSSIBILITY OF A TRAP NOT FULLY EXCLUDED, AS THIS MAY BE A SET-UP AGAINST THE VERY VERY IMPORTANT POLITICAL PERSON. FORCE COMMANDER TO INFORM SRSG FIRST THING IN MORNING TO ENSURE HIS SUPPORT.

12. PEUX CE QUE VEUX. ALLONS-Y.

Figure 4.2

other hand, emphasised that the one basic premise for the operation, namely the ceasefire, was holding and ultimately Resolution 909 was adopted by the UNSC on 5 April 1994, detailing an extension of UNAMIR's mandate and implementation of the Arusha Peace Agreement. Nevertheless, Resolution 909 stated that UNAMIR would be removed from Rwanda in six weeks unless the BBTG was created. This has to be interpreted with due consideration to other ongoing global circumstances during February and March of 1994, namely the renewed conflict in Bosnia with mortar shells targeting the Sarajevo central market (Smith 1994); US forces were departing Somalia (Stevenson 1995); and the North Korean nuclear issue was causing concern in Asia (Tyler 1994). Wheeler notes that the GOR was not unaware of these global concerns:

> It is one of those cruel ironies that Rwanda was a member of the Council at this time and hence its Ambassador was well aware of the reluctance of the USA to support the continuation of UNAMIR. Even a cursory glance at

> Resolution 909 would have done nothing to make the extremists think that the UN was prepared to intervene forcibly against them.
>
> (Wheeler 2000: 217)

It is therefore arguable that, between 1990 and early 1994, having endured three years of murderous civil war and violent multiparty politics, Rwanda was in a deep, protean and escalating crisis. A nominal coalition government existed, with the opposition holding key posts, but in reality there was a major political impasse (Gasana 2002: 240, 250). A peace agreement was in place, but both government forces and the RPF were rearming and preparing for war (ibid: 243–4).

The catalyst for genocide

The catalyst for the genocide was a complex and disputed sequence of events, which began with the 1990 incursion into northern Rwanda by the RPF army, continued throughout the Arusha Accords conference in Tanzania (June 1992–August 1993) and ended with the shooting down of President Juvénal Habyarimana's plane on 6 April 1994 when one surface-to-air missile (SAM) struck one of the wings of the aircraft and a second missile hit its tail. The plane erupted into flames in mid-air before crashing into the garden of the presidential palace and exploding on impact, killing all on board (Dallaire 2004: 221–4).The plane carried three French crew and nine passengers including the President of Burundi, thus bringing to three the number of Hutu Presidents killed within a six-month period.

As we have established, prior to this assassination, Rwanda was a country poised on a knife-edge, staggering from one near catastrophe to another whilst chaos reigned. Habyarimana was under explicit, escalating pressure from increasingly impatient international sponsors and leaders of neighbouring countries to implement the transfer of power to the BBTG. 'Foreign pressure became intense' (Prunier 1995/2002: 209). The 'final talking-to' was to be administered to Habyarimana by leaders from Uganda, Kenya, Burundi, the United Nations and other international brokers of the peace process, at a meeting arranged by Tanzania's President, and set for 6 April in Dar Es Salaam. Under extreme pressure, Habyarimana at last agreed at the meeting of 6 April to move to implementation of the previously agreed power-sharing arrangement. It was on his return flight and on approach to the landing runaway of Kigali airport that his French Mystère Falcon jet, a gift from President Mitterrand of France, was shot down (ibid: 211–12).

There is no disagreement amongst scholars and commentators that the assassination of President Habyarimana was the critical turning point in the sequence of events that led to the unrestrained mass killings of Rwandese and exodus of refugees from Rwanda. However, to this day, no official investigation has been launched into the attack on the plane or the death of its occupants and as such no individual, group or organisation has been convicted of responsibility. Immediately after the death of Habyarimana, there was widespread speculation by outside Anglophone analysts of an *akazu*-sponsored plot 'to prevent the BBTG being installed' (Gaillard and Barrada 1994: 12–19; Eltringham 2004: 111). Meanwhile, the Hutu hardliners[9] used radio stations to incite Hutu citizens to avenge the death of the Rwandese President, claiming that 'the Belgians or the RPF had definitely shot down the plane' (Chalk 2000: 101). The day following the assassination of Habyarimana, 10 Belgian UN peacekeepers were murdered by Rwandan soldiers who, as a result of hate propaganda, believed them to have been involved in the shooting down of the aircraft (ibid: 102).

Until recent times, the consensus of Anglophone literature has held that the Hutu hardliners of Rwanda pursued genocide to keep power and that the genocide had specific, powerful architects who were members of the *akazu*. Scholars and human rights activists emphasised, in the first few years following the atrocity, that these hardliners planned the genocide for some considerable time before it happened (Prunier 1995/2002: 169; Des Forges 1999: 5) with Pottier referring to 'a masterplan for the extermination of Habyarimana's political opponents and all Tutsi … a plan already in existence in 1993' (2002: 31). Indeed Linda Melvern produced an entire book, *Conspiracy to Murder* (2004), attesting to the pre-planned genocide by the Rwandan ruling elite. Contradicting such claims was the post-genocide Francophone literature that negated the responsibility of the Hutu ruling elite in either the assassination of Habyarimana or in pre-planning of genocide in Rwanda. Péan alleges the existence of counter-genocide, and both he and Ruzibiza[10] point to the heavy responsibility of President Paul Kagame in creating the conditions that led to the ghastly carnage (2005). Shortly after the plane was downed, French military officers in Kigali met Dallaire, who as Force Commander of UNAMIR was responsible for airport security, and offered to investigate the assassination. France was particularly concerned by the event since the plane belonged to France and French nationals had been killed; moreover, French investigators were available nearby. In his testimony as a prosecution witness at the ICTR, General Dallaire confirmed that he had refused the French offer because he had already discussed the issue with the Americans, who were prepared to dispatch an investigating team from their bases in Germany.[11]

On 8 April 1994, the UNSC demanded an impartial international inquiry into the assassination. On 12 April, the Belgian Cabinet also demanded the International Civil Aviation Organization conduct an investigation. A document distributed by the Uganda Democratic Coalition on 12 April[12] to foreign embassies and journalists some six days after the assassination of Habyarimana accused the Pentagon of being 'conspirators with dictator Museveni and RPF leaders in the assassination plot' (UDC, cited in Prunier 1995/2002: 216). On 25 June, the UNSC mandated the Secretary-General to conduct an inquiry into the assassination. In November 1994, the UNSC created the ICTR with the mandate to investigate acts of genocide or other serious violations of international human rights law committed on Rwandan territory during the year 1994. In September 1995, Zaire demanded that an inquiry be held into the assassination, as did Kenyan President Arap Moi in October.

Alternate versions, rumour and speculation have thrived throughout the 18-year period since Habyarimana's death. Despite two presidents having been assassinated, to this day, no official international inquiry has been conducted into the killings. This lack of investigation prompted Belgian Professor Filip Reyntjens to conclude that 'in fact, nobody seems to really want to know' who assassinated the two Presidents. Reyntjens maintained that all the evidence available tended to incriminate the RPF (Reyntjens 1995: 46–7).

In the shadow of the plane crash – the response of the Hutu extremists

During the night of 6–7 April 1994, in the immediate aftermath of the plane crash, roadblocks were thrown up both in and around Kigali by both the Rwandan army and members of the *Interahamwe* militia. Targeted killings of opposition leaders began. Most notable among the first of those who died trying to escape was the Prime Minister, Agathe Uwilingiyimana, an MDR moderate (Dallaire 2004: 245). Indeed, it was while endeavouring to escort her to safety that 10 Belgian paratroopers were captured, disarmed and later butchered by Rwandan government forces, an action which led a few days later to the withdrawal of the entire Belgian contingent from UNAMIR (ibid: 236–57). In an interview with Agnes Ntamabyariro (2005), a pre-genocide Rwandan Justice Minister revealed that later the same night, with the president and his advisors dead, and few Government ministers remaining in the country, an assortment of Hutu extremist leaders, including the interviewee, gathered together to form an 'interim government' in which she played an instrumental role. Chief architect of the process of putting together the new administration that night was Colonel Théoneste Bagosora, a leading member of the *akazu*.

In the immediate aftermath of the plane crash, the RPF remained somewhat detached, albeit monitoring the situation closely and maintaining communications with UNAMIR staff (Dallaire 2004: 234). Tito Rutemara, an RPF diplomat stationed at the CND building in Kigali with the 600 RPF troops, nevertheless delivered an unambiguous threat to UNAMIR: 'If the killing does not stop, our troops will be forced to attack' (Interview with Rutemara, Rwanda, 2005). Kagame contacted Dallaire from Mulindi on the morning of 7 April saying that his people inside the capital were at risk and steps must be taken to protect them. He later sent a message to Dallaire that stated, 'I have just learned many homes of our supporters are surrounded by RPF soldiers. The intention's certainly clear. Informing you that our forces have to react to protect ours. I'm very serious and want to info you before [*sic*]' (Dallaire 2004: 245). Moderate politicians and members of the general public continued throughout the day to be removed from their houses and killed whilst others were being attacked on the streets and at the roadblocks.

Later in the afternoon of 7 April, Kagame messaged Dallaire for a third time, this time with a straightforward ultimatum indicating that he would order his troops to intervene if the killings did not cease immediately. More specifically, Kagame indicated that the RPF would launch an attack should the situation not be secured by last light on 7 April. It was at this time unlikely that UNAMIR had the ability to bring the situation under control (ibid: 247). The Commander of the 2,700-strong UNAMIR force called for urgent reinforcements for his troops and an immediate change of mandate from the existing passive 'peacekeeping' Chapter VI role to one that would empower UNAMIR to enforce peace and intervene to save lives. His request was refused (Interview with Dallaire, London, 2005). Shortly thereafter, Kagame launched 'a well-planned offensive' (Waugh 2004: 67), violating UN-monitored ceasefire lines 'in a bid to restore order' (Peterson 2001: 254).

Europeans evacuate Rwanda: Operation Amaryllis

On 9 April, and having given Dallaire only 40 minutes of prior notice, French troops landed at Kigali Airport with the explicit intention of evacuating French nationals from the country (Interview with Dallaire, London 2005). Problematic to the French evacuation are the allegations that upon landing in Kigali, weapons destined for Hutu extremists and militia were unloaded from the plane before French nationals and members of the family of the deceased Habyarimana could embark. Such actions by the French are explored in detail in Chapter 6. The evacuation was conducted effectively and rapidly with the last French troops leaving on 14 April. The Belgians had begun a similar operation out of Nairobi on 10 April whilst the United States sent about 300 troops to neighbouring Burundi for the same purpose, but did not enter Rwanda. Instead, US civilians were escorted to the border by UNAMIR and airlifted from there.

By 10 April, the fourth day of massacres, Dallaire was able to conclude that what he was witnessing was no longer just a politically motivated massacre but an immense campaign of torture and murder against anybody carrying a Tutsi identity card (Interview with Dallaire, London, 2005). The resumption of the 'civil war' commenced in the early hours of 13 April, one week after the assassination of Habyarimana and the day before the departure of the French troops who were evacuating their nationals. Over the course of a few hours, 2,400 RPF militia had infiltrated Kigali and joined the 600 RPF soldiers stationed within the CND Parliament building. A further critical factor was the decision by the Belgian Government, formally announced on 14 April, to withdraw its battalion from UNAMIR. The Belgian contingent was by far the best equipped and best trained unit seconded to UNAMIR. British Foreign Secretary Douglas Hurd telephoned his Belgian counterpart in an effort to encourage the government to reverse its decision but to no avail (Interview, London, 2006). The withdrawal began on 19 April and was completed the following day.

Reaction to continuing pleas from UNAMIR

For two weeks after 6 April, the UNSC held almost daily consultations on the Rwanda crisis. During the first week there was little consistency in the discussions, compounded by the fact that the advice that was coming from the Special Representative of the Secretary-General (SRSG) in Kigali, Jacques-Roger Booh-Booh, was that the ongoing violence in Rwanda was due to the resumption of the civil war. Colin Keating, President of the UNSC, felt that 'this was transparently not the case … and so there was a disconnect between the political advice that was coming from the SRSG and the realities of the situation' (Interview, New York, 2006).

The message that UNAMIR had to be strengthened if it was to have any impact on the ground was communicated to the UNSC on numerous occasions. On 19 April, during the final drafting of the Secretary-General's report to the UNSC, the DPKO representative argued that the UNAMIR force was unable to function, and there was no prospect of a ceasefire in Rwanda. At no time was there any attempt to deconstruct the violence into its two distinct parts: the fighting between the RPF and the forces of the interim government; and the massacres being carried out by individuals or lightly armed militias against unarmed civilians (Wheeler 2000).

As such, the Secretary-General presented the option of a sharp withdrawal from Rwanda as a strong recommendation to the UNSC, albeit not negating the provision of a massive reinforcement for UNAMIR as an alternative option (Barnett 2002: 117). In his report to the UNSC of 20 April, the Secretary-General underlined that the UNAMIR personnel 'cannot be left at risk indefinitely when there is no possibility for their performing the tasks for which they were dispatched'. Thus, on 21 April, in the midst of unabated genocide, the UNSC agreed on Resolution 912, reducing UNAMIR to 270 troops. In the UNSC, isolated voices appealed for troops, but their words were drowned out by those advocating withdrawal. Barnett asserts that in reaching such a decision 'the United States used its considerable power in the Security Council to help muzzle the call for intervention and later obstructed those who wanted to intervene' (ibid: 2). The decision to withdraw the main bulk of the peacekeeping force was met with criticism from several quarters, including the Organization of African Unity (OAU), which denounced the withdrawal as 'a sign of indifference or lack of sufficient concern' for Africans (Leitenberg 1994). The Secretary-General's reasons were many, including the simple fact of a lack of available of troops for intervention. However, this is disputed by Keating, who stated: 'Resources could have been made available for an operation reinforcing UNAMIR in May 1994, but resources were not the problem. The problem was a lack of political will' (Interview, New York, 2006). A political officer within the United Nations during this period of time has suggested that the Secretariat sanitised much of the communications arriving at the United Nations from Dallaire, 'because it did not want to encourage an intervention' (Barnett 2002: 118). One can only speculate about alternative reasons for such deviance.

On 29 April, the Secretary-General's letter to the President of the UNSC appealed to the UNSC to take more forceful action to stop the continuing massacres in Rwanda. This initiative marked a shift of focus and direction in the Secretary-General's attitude towards the Rwandan crisis with the Secretary-General informing the UNSC:

> that the Force Commander of the United Nations Assistance Mission for Rwanda has reported a further deterioration of the situation in Kigali and other parts of Rwanda ... UNAMIR reports strong evidence of preparations for further massacres of civilians in the city and there are several large concentrations of civilians who fear for their lives but enjoy little effective protection.
>
> (UN Doc S/1994/518)

Having updated the UNSC on the seriousness of the situation in Rwanda, the Secretary-General continued:

> I urge the Security Council to re-examine the decisions which it took in resolution 912 and to consider again what action, including forceful action, it could take, or could authorize Member States to take, in order to restore law and order and end the massacres. In making this recommendation, I am of course aware that such action would require a commitment of human and material resources on a scale, which Member States have so far proved reluctant to contemplate. But I am convinced that the scale of human suffering in Rwanda and its implications for the stability of neighbouring countries leaves the Security Council with no alternative but to examine this possibility
>
> (ibid)

Authorising the expansion of UNAMIR

With no Western state willing to commit troops to an expanded UNAMIR, the United Nations's only alternative was to create a strengthened force comprising of African troops with Western financial and logistical support. Resolution 918 was duly adopted as of 17 May 1994, which saw the UNSC adjust the mandate for UNAMIR and increase its strength to 5,500 troops. Following most of the recommendations of the Secretary-General, UNAMIR II would support and provide safe conditions for displaced persons and other groups in Rwanda and would help with the provision of assistance by humanitarian organizations. UNAMIR II would also monitor border-crossing points and, though the operation's rules of engagement did not include enforcement action, UNAMIR was authorized under Chapter VI of the UN Charter to proactively protect civilians. The UNSC solved this apparent inconsistency by introducing an expanded definition of 'self-defence' in Resolution 918: the force could be 'required to take action in self-defence against those who threatened protected sites and populations and the means of delivery and distribution of humanitarian relief' (ibid). Until this time, similar protection mandates in UN operations – notably the 'no fly zone' and 'safe havens' in Bosnia, and the humanitarian zone in Northern Iraq – had been based on Chapter VII.

The United States had reservations about the proposal, which it interpreted as establishing a large peace enforcement mission to restore order and pacify the population of Rwanda. As such, it called for a small force restricted to merely monitoring the borders. The United States finally agreed to the Secretary-General's concept but insisted on phased deployment, with only the first phase being implemented until a functioning cease-fire was in place. Such US conditionality governed the entire process of establishing the expanded operation, and significantly delayed the process. The American insistence of phased deployment was criticised by several UNSC members, as well as by Boutros-Ghali and General Dallaire (Interviews, 2005–06).

DPKO officials spent the following months in endless negotiations trying to source logistics and equipment from Western countries. The combination of excessive demands from the African troop-contributing countries and a lack of response from Western countries made the deployment of UNAMIR II a slow and difficult task (Adelman and Suhrke 1996). At a press conference in New York, 25 May 1994, the Secretary-General intimated that 'more than 200,000 people have been killed and the international community is still discussing what ought to be done. I have tried. I was in contact with different Heads of State, and I begged them to send troops' (UN Doc SG/SM/5292).

In his report, released some six days later, the UN Secretary-General reported that:

> The magnitude of the human calamity that has engulfed Rwanda might be unimaginable but for its having transpired. On the basis of the evidence that has emerged, there can be little doubt that it constitutes genocide, since there have been large-scale killings of communities and families belonging to a particular ethnic group.
>
> (ibid)

Some two weeks after the authorisation of Phase 1 of Resolution 918, namely to strengthen UNAMIR to 800 troops, no troops had yet arrived in Rwanda. The Government of Ghana was prepared to dispatch the required troops immediately; however, the Secretary-General noted in his report of 31 May 1994:

> they can be deployed only when essential equipment, especially armoured personnel carriers, is provided and moved to Rwanda. Without equipment, the troops would be unprotected, immobile and ineffective. … It is estimated that phase 1 will not be operational for another four to six weeks depending on how soon the resources required are made available by Member States and delivered on the ground.
>
> (UN Doc S/1994/640)

Despite Ghana being prepared to provide troops, the Secretary-General made it clear that there was a desperate need for equipment so as to allow the troops to be deployed and phase 1 to be implemented, a deployment which would hopefully put an end to the genocidal massacres still on going in Rwanda. The Secretary-General was desperate for equipment, air support and armoured personnel carriers (APCs) but the difficulties in his requests can be seen as his report continues:

> It is unacceptable that, almost two months since this violence exploded, killings still continue. … The delay in reaction by the international community to the genocide in Rwanda has demonstrated graphically its extreme inadequacy to respond urgently with prompt and decisive action to humanitarian crises entwined with armed conflict. Having quickly reduced UNAMIR to a minimal presence on the ground, since its original mandate did not allow it to take action when the carnage started, the international community appears paralysed in reacting almost two months later even to the revised mandate established by the Security Council.
>
> (ibid)

In a letter from the Secretary-General to the President of the UNSC dated 19 June 1994, the Secretary-General reported on continuing difficulties he was continuing to encounter in obtaining medical and other support units. 'It should be noted that none of those Governments possessing the capacity to provide fully trained and equipped military units have offered so far to do so … Meanwhile the situation in Rwanda has continued to deteriorate and the killing of innocent civilians has not stopped' (UN Doc S/1994/728).

As the genocidal killings continued throughout Rwanda in 1994, the French Government put forward a resolution to the United Nations offering to undertake a humanitarian intervention in Rwanda. This resolution was adopted and as a result Operation Turquoise was launched within a few hours. This UN supported intervention is subject to analysis in Chapter 5.

Fighting between the RPF and GOR forces in Kigali continued until 4 July 1994 when RPF forces took control of the northern part of the city, and brought most of the fighting in the city to a halt. After having taken military control over most of the country, the RPF decided to end the war on 18 July 1994 by declaring unilaterally a cease-fire and establishing a 'Government of National Unity' the following day.[13]

In the immediate aftermath of the genocide, countless studies, reports and commissions have examined the United Nations's response, attempting to piece together what happened and ultimately to determine whom to blame for the abandonment of the people of Rwanda. On the whole, responsibility has been placed firmly on the shoulders of the US Government (for example, see Power 2002). A subsequent wave of investigations revealed, however, a much more complex story, shifting responsibility towards the permanent members of the UNSC, which clearly includes the United States, and the Secretariat (see for example Adelman and Suhrke 1996). Des Forges (1999: 625–8) also sharply illustrated the way in which the UNSC concentrated on the civil war as opposed to the genocide. The UNSC was solely concerned with the question of how UNAMIR could assist in obtaining a cease-fire, but rarely touched upon the fate of Rwandans or how UNAMIR could respond to the crimes against humanity being perpetrated (Interviews, London, 2005–06). The ceasefire talks had, without exception, ended in stalemate.

Decision-making processes: 'Somalia is absolutely central'

It is widely acknowledged in the literature, and also established through interviews undertaken for this study, that the decision-making process throughout the period of the genocide in Rwanda was complicated by the 'Mogadishu Factor' which had given negative connotations to both the terms 'humanitarian intervention' and 'peace enforcement'. The 'Mogadishu Factor' refers to the early 1990s when the UNSC voted to confront a situation in Somalia in which civil order had totally collapsed and warring clans had seized control of the country.[14] On 5 June 1993, 23 Pakistani peacekeepers were ambushed and killed in the Somalian capital of Mogadishu by members of a Somali militia, which led the United States to launch a unilateral intervention. On 3 October 1993, 18 US Army Rangers from this operation were also killed in Mogadishu while attempting to apprehend Somali militia leaders. Television footage of a Ranger's body being dragged through the streets of Mogadishu prompted a public outcry in the United States that soon led to the withdrawal of all US forces from Somalia and the subsequent collapse of the UN-led and US-led operations. Ironically, the US troops had remained under US command and control at all times with the United Nations simply providing a legal basis for their presence in Somalia and legitimising their actions (Wheeler 2000: 178–200).

Interviewees indicate that America's 'Somalia experience', some six months prior to the commencement of the genocide in Rwanda, substantially diminished political will in the United States and elsewhere to engage in military interventions for purely humanitarian purposes. 'There was a lack of political will to take another risk in Africa' (Interview with former British Ambassador to the UNSC, London, 2006). Somalia constituted an important precedent for the international rules on the use of force. For the first time, the UNSC had deemed a human rights crisis a threat to the peace and used its Chapter VII powers to authorise military intervention for the sole purpose of preventing further suffering.

Several former Ambassadors to the United Nations believe that one simply cannot begin to understand how Rwanda happened without considering the events that occurred in Somalia in October 1993. In a 2006 interview, one former Ambassador stated:

> Somalia is absolutely central to all this, the experience of Somalia, the intervention that took place there with the support of everybody in the world, and all the Africans, the big military force deployed in Somalia, the collapse following the killing of the Americans, the withdrawal of the mission, which came only a few months before Rwanda in which the UN peacekeepers slunk away with their tail between their legs and Somalia was virtually left to its own devices, basically insoluble. ... It doesn't justify what happened nor indeed was the parallel as close as many people at the time thought it was – I do not believe for one second that had there been a massive intervention in Rwanda it would have got into as much trouble as the one in Somalia – I do not think that it would. But if you are asking why was it that Governments couldn't bring themselves to respond positively to the Secretary General when he went to them after the killing started and when the first two battalions – the Bangladeshis and the Belgians – had departed and said 'I need more troops', they all found reasons why they couldn't provide them.
>
> (ibid)

According to Power (2002: 332), 'most in the Pentagon greeted the news of the Belgians' death as proof that the UN mission in Rwanda had gone from being a "Somalia waiting to happen" to a "Somalia that was happening".

Media portrayal: ancient tribal feuds

It was some time after the start of the genocide before the interplay of the tragedy's multiple causes became clear to the majority of media workers, although there were still some notable exceptions. Lindsey Hilsum was one of very few journalists in the country as the violence erupted and described how 'the streets were piling high with bodies. There was killing, chaos, an orgy of Rwandan blood that had erupted like a grenade blast inside an overripe melon' (cited in Peterson 2001: 253).

Despite Hilsum's best efforts, surveys have shown the reporting on the killings in Rwanda was generally portrayed as ancient tribal feuds. Indeed, Pottier has highlighted how '[t]he thin line between information and disinformation blurs in times of conflict and war, all the more so when fighting restricts access to regions and their people' (2002: 53), and such was the case in Rwanda. Indeed, the major analytical themes of the new consensus are far removed from the original model of ancient tribal hatred. Rather than seeing the violence as chaotic frenzy, as state failure or as an explosion of atavistic animosities, scholars and human rights activists alike stress that the violence was modern, systematic and intentional.

When the genocide accelerated, the Western press virtually ceased to report on Rwanda (Hilsum 1995; Johansson 1995; Livingston and Eachus 1995). This lack of coverage cannot be blamed simply on the relative disinterest in Rwanda. The real danger, the genuine confusion on the ground, the restricted mobility of reporters, and the inability to fly out photos or videos were all major handicaps. In addition, American media organisations had ordered their reporters out for reasons of safety, and possibly also because of cost (Adelman and Suhrke 1996: 46). However, as one critic remarked, 'the massacre in Rwanda was not sudden at all, but the culmination of years of trouble, which the press for the most part did not cover' (MacGuire 1994, cited in Livingston and Eachus 2000: 215). Nor did they understand the context, which left them vulnerable to powerful manipulation.

The civil war and genocide that blighted Rwanda caused much of its population to be internally displaced and enormous crowds to flee to surrounding countries. With the RPF's takeover in mid-July 1994, and with the encouragement of extremist radio, Rwandans implicated in the genocide, their relatives, and those who feared the arrival of the RPF, all fled to neighbouring countries. On 13 July, a stretch of road less than 60km long in the north of Rwanda had more than a million refugees walking along it. By 18 July, more than a million people had crossed the border into Zaire in less than a week. Large numbers of Rwandans, especially Tutsi survivors of the genocide, had lost all they possessed, including their houses. However, it must also be acknowledged that members of the RPF and the increasingly massive influx of Tutsi returnees coming partly from Uganda but more frequently Burundi, were also responsible on occasion for misappropriating the homes of survivors of genocide. Those returning to the country were met with gruesome sights. 'Bodies lay everywhere' (Interview with Felix, Rwanda, 2005), 'people were dying on the roadsides and no one stopped to help' (Interview with Emmanuel, Rwanda, 2005). For those who fled Rwanda, the refugee camps in Tanzania and Goma, Zaire, were 'living versions of hell' (Interview with Rose, Rwanda, 2005). It was these scenes that attracted wide-scale media attention and as a result, most news coverage of Rwanda came in July and August 1994; the focus was wholly devoted to Goma, where 1.2 million refugees, mostly Hutu, were ravaged by dehydration, cholera and dysentery. Compared to the inherent dangers of Rwanda for the previous few months, Goma provided an easy-to-film spectacle of grotesque suffering and death in real time.

A judicial statement: rejecting the theory of conspiracy to commit genocide

On 18 December 2008, a three judge panel in the Military I case at the ICTR:[15]

> … completely rejected the Prosecution theory of long-term planning and conspiracy to commit genocide by members of the former Rwandan military leadership. All four defendants were found 'not guilty' of all counts charging conspiracy to commit genocide, based on the Chambers ruling that their actions prior to April 6, 1994 were based on war-time conditions, not planning to kill civilians or to carry out a genocide against Tutsi Rwandans.
>
> (ICTR Press Office 2008)

Three of the four defendants in the Military I trial were, however, convicted of crimes of genocide (ibid). It should be noted that the ICTR defence in the Military I trial was based on previously suppressed contemporaneous UN and declassified US documents, which identify the RPF as the war-time aggressor responsible for massive chaos within Rwanda throughout 1994, violence that was initiated by their four-year war of invasion from Uganda by Kagame's RPF army (Erlinder 2009).

The judgments have caused one academic to ask:

> If there was no conspiracy and no planning to kill ethnic civilians, can the tragedy that engulfed Rwanda properly be called "a genocide" at all? Or, was it closer to a case of civilians being caught up in war-time violence, like the Eastern Front in WWII, rather than the planned behind-the-lines killings in Nazi death camps? The ICTR judgment found the former.
>
> (Erlinder 2008)

There are to date no absolute certainties about who killed President Habyarimana, nor about the exact purpose of his assassination, although those acquitted of conspiracy to commit genocide at the Military I trials were accused directly by the prosecution of the missile attack during their trial. However, in the concluding judgments of the trial, the ICTR specifically referred to evidence presented to the Chamber that 'civilian killings in Rwanda were triggered by the assassination of the Rwandan President, which was part of the final assault to seize power by the RPF army of Paul

Kagame in 1994' (ICTR Press Office 2008). This finding supports evidence, established by Hourigan and described as very detailed and very credible, which 'corroborated some other information ... learnt from Alison Des Forges the week before'.[16] Interviews undertaken with prisoners convicted of genocide established their unified belief that the genocide committed by the Hutu of Rwanda was a spontaneous expression of popular anger at the death of their president rather than the meticulously planned and brilliantly administered conspiracy we had been led to believe by the Anglophone journalists such as Keane (1996), Gourevitch (2000) and Melvern (2000) who maintain an RPF-friendly stance.

The judgments of the ICTR led the President of Human Rights Watch to write an open letter to the Justice Hassan B. Jallow, the current ICTR Prosecutor, calling for the ICTR to fulfil its mandate by holding Kagame, and his RPF regime, accountable for crimes committed in 1994 in Rwanda (Waldorf 2011).

Was the genocide preventable or stoppable? A hypothetical intervention

Kuperman states that 'there is a growing consensus among American policy-makers that humanitarian military intervention should be launched to stop genocide when such violence comes to light, especially where intervention can save lives at low cost' (2001: 100). But could lives have been saved in Rwanda? Barnett argues that 'what sets the Rwandan genocide apart from all other genocide is that the international community could have intervened at relatively low cost before the effects were fully realized' (Barnett 2002: 1). Kuperman agrees that intervention could have saved lives, but argues that 'a realistic US military intervention launched as soon as President Clinton could have determined that genocide was being attempted in Rwanda would not have averted the genocide' (2001: 109). Irrespective of political will for the use of force, Straus argues that a 'swift and decisive' international intervention would have prevented mass murder by 'short-circuit[ing] some of the dynamics driving the violence' saving hundreds of thousands of lives (2006: 241). Further, in an independent report commissioned by the OAU, a conclusion was reached that the permanent members of the UNSC could have prevented the genocide from taking place, adding 'this was the most easily preventable genocide imaginable' (OAU 2000). Other commentators have also insisted that with a modest increase in troops and capabilities – which had been requested in the first week of the genocide – UNAMIR could have prevented most of the killings (Dallaire 2004: 514; Stanton 2004: 224). Indeed, Des Forges has argued that diplomatic intervention alone would have been sufficient to prevent the genocide, since Rwanda was heavily dependent on foreign financial support and any Rwandan government committing genocide would have reacted to a threat to halt aid (Des Forges 1999: 24–6, 641). This begs the question of why there was no such intervention. Contrary to academic consensus, the former British Ambassador to the UNSC, Sir David Hannay, is 'convinced that there was nothing the UN could have done to prevent the genocide in Rwanda' (Interview, London, 2006). The President of the UNSC of April 1994 indicates that:

> Rwandans [the interim Government] were totally aware of the dynamics within the Council ... and so it would have been extremely difficult for the Council to have collectively managed a prevention operation. However, an intervention could have significantly interrupted the progress and mitigated the death toll ... but in fact for two months the US was not willing to agree to deploy additional troops by which time it was too late.
>
> (Interview with Keating, New York, 2006)

On 21 July, US President Clinton promised a vigorous US approach to the refugee problem in Zaire with a $76m budget and a large number of transport planes from bases in Germany.

Chapter 5

The French 'Resolution': 'Considerable Political and Geostrategic Interests are Hidden Behind the Rwandese Heap of Corpses'

This book notes that despite historical evidence of Western state complicity in genocide in periods of European colonialism and war, there have been limited scholarly efforts to conceptualise compliance in such atrocities. Open discussions of Western institutional complicity are therefore key to facilitate a genuine and reflective debate, and as such, having undertaken a macro study of Britain's role in the Rwandan genocide, I feel it is helpful to allude to current debates in relation to French complicity in the Rwandan genocide and to describe a micro case study of French complicity in the mountainous region of Bisesero in 1994.

French policy in post-independence Africa

Among the former colonial powers that once ruled Africa, France is the only country to have continued, post-independence, to station its own troops in Africa, constituting what has been described as a 'permanent intervention' (Luckham 1982: 56). France is the only ex-colonial power that retains defence treaties, military agreements and complex systems of military co-operation with its former colonies – almost half of Africa's 54 recognised states. France has also generated strong relationships with Francophone African countries that were not colonies of France prior to independence, as in Rwanda where France nurtured a relationship with Juvénal Habyarimana from the beginning of his presidency in 1973 (McNulty 2000). Prunier believes that France perceives itself 'as a large hen followed by a docile brood of little black chicks' (1995/2002: 103).

French policy towards Africa has witnessed recurrent and controversial military interventions on the African continent since decolonisation. The intricacies of Franco-African accords and agreements, and political and economic involvement has 'enabled the French army to intervene at least thirty times in Africa since 1963' (Martin 1995: 13). Martin also notes that 'a number of *coup d'états* have occurred in various Francophone countries [in Africa] precisely when French economic, political and strategic interests were being directly or indirectly threatened', and that Giscard d'Estaing,

French President 1974–81, revealed in the French newspaper *Le Monde* that '[w]e have intervened in Africa whenever an unacceptable situation had to be remedied' (1985: 194), confirming that such agreements reek of neo-colonial control of Francophone Africa.[1]

The projection of French culture and values overseas is integral to French foreign policy and France protects its global status in equal proportion to the requirement for French patronage of African elites (Kroslak 2007). In addition, France has depended on Africa as a source of strategic raw materials[2] (Martin 1985), as a market for its manufactured goods and as an outlet for capital investment (Martin 1995).

There is a long history of Francophone and Anglophone rivalry in Africa, most particularly in the Congo-Zaire region. French fears of losing influence and exclusivity in Francophone Africa to Anglo-Saxon states[3] were fuelled by an identity crisis in French foreign policy as a result of increased Cold War tensions between France and the United States in other geopolitical areas and, some say, the memory of the Fashoda incident in 1898,[4] since when 'the French had been watchful in guarding against Anglophone intrusion in what they considered to be their own backyard – *le pré carré*' (Prunier 1995/2002: 99).

French foreign policy in the Great Lakes region during the Cold War indeed demonstrates a genuine fear that Anglophone states would supplant French influence in the Congo. Debates continue into the validity of such 'Anglo-Saxon' conspiracy theories (Huliaras 2003: 297). Yet according to the memoirs of Jacques Foccart[5] (1995/1997), it was the successful efforts of the United States in giving power to the pro-American Mobutu Sese Seko in the Congo in 1965 that facilitated the penetration of 'Anglo-Saxon influence' into the largest country of Francophone Africa, constituting a clear victory for the United States at the expense of French interests. According to Bayart (1995), contemporary French Anglophobia is motivated not so much by a threat from the United Kingdom as it is by the previously noted unpalatable extension of American influence on the African continent. Smith even describes 'a highly public duel between Paris and Washington in Francophone Africa' (1994: 355–67).

Western actors have been of central importance to Rwandan society throughout the twentieth century, shaping its economy, its social relations and its political power structure. When Juvénal Habyarimana was elected to the Presidency of Rwanda in 1973, d'Estaing's right-wing French Government soon became Habyarimana's closest military and political ally. The relationship developed and resulted in the signing of a Franco–Rwandan military co-operation and training agreement in Paris in 1975 (Prunier 1995/2002: 89n). Some speculated that such relationships were being nurtured by the French in Francophone Africa to counter the perceived rise of Anglo-Saxon influence on the continent in the shadow of decolonisation (Kroslak 2007). The 1975 agreement stated, 'The Government of the French Republic places at the disposal of the government of the Rwandese republic the French military personnel whose services are required for the organisation and instruction of the Rwandese national police' (McNulty 2000: 109). In 1978, the OAU spoke out against the existence of foreign military bases on the African continent, but despite such condemnation, the French military persisted, maintaining 400 *coopérant* forces in Rwanda throughout the 1980s. Such external influence made Rwanda one of the most externally controlled states in the world among non-communist countries. The Franco–Rwandan relationship was further strengthened when d'Estaing was succeeded in 1981 by the socialist president, François François Mitterrand (Des Forges 1999).

Mitterrand and 'the hissing snake in the garden of Eden'

> Mitterrand's policy in Africa was consistent with his Machiavellian outlook on politics and his cynical regard for life in general.
>
> (Wallis 2006: 20)

Mitterrand's presidential campaign promoted a 'new way' in France's view of the world and an ethical foreign policy that 'pledged to defend the rights of the oppressed people everywhere, to champion a fairer system of international development and work for world disarmament' (Cole 1997: 140). He portrayed himself as an ardent supporter of reducing France's sale of armaments, stating that France should instead aim to export goods that would not further destabilise the developing world with the threat of civil or international war in the way that armaments do. Endorsing such a foreign policy was problematic given that, at Mitterand's inauguration in 1981, France was the leading arms exporter per capita in the world.[6] Mitterrand's policy of supporting the 'poor and oppressed' was truly short-lived, however; arms sales to despots with dreadful human rights records thrived (Wallis 2006: 20), and Mitterrand continued to propagate a close military relationship with the Habyarimana's Rwandan dictatorship (Des Forges 1999).

The fall of the Berlin Wall in 1989 signalled the end of the Cold War and the replacement of hitherto fairly complementary US and French foreign policies with a new competitive international environment in which American and French policies were both clearly being driven by economic self-interest (Schraeder 2000). Indeed, 1992 witnessed a myriad of American public speeches denoting a considerable deviation from its Cold War tendency to defer to European economic interests in their former colonies, in favour of a more belligerent US approach in the promotion of US trade and investment in Africa (ibid).

Much of France's post-Cold-War policy towards Rwanda appears to have been motivated by this reform to US foreign policy in Africa. In supporting the regime of Habyarimana, the French saw the opportunity to defeat the rising forces of 'the hissing snake in the Garden of Eden' (Prunier 1995/2002: 104), namely the Anglophone RPF guerrilla force based in Uganda, which was formed from Rwandan Tutsi exiles in opposition to the Francophone regime in Rwanda. The French Government was resolute in its portrayal of the RPF as synonymous with the Ugandan army of Museveni, which it rightly accused of arming and training the guerrilla force. Being Anglophone, and with a strong allegiance to the United Kingdom, the French considered Museveni to be the very personification of an Anglo-Saxon agent, and viewed as a great threat to Francophone Africa.

The little chicks call on the large hen – Operation Noroît

The RPF invasion of Rwanda on 1 October 1990 was somewhat unanticipated by Habyarimana, who was attending an event in New York in the company of his arch-enemy President Museveni of Uganda. Shortly after the invasion, Habyarimana directed a plea for urgent French military assistance to President Mitterrand, voicing his alarm and his fears of an Anglophone Tutsi plot to carve out a large new central African kingdom. This resulted in the immediate launch of French Operation Noroît to Rwanda and dramatic increases in French military numbers in the country, radically altering the nature and extent of the military relationship between France and Rwanda. The official reason given for Mitterrand's decision to launch Operation Noroît was for the protection of French expatriates in Rwanda in the event of continuing unrest. However, Kroslak (2007) evidences that from the beginning of the outbreak of civil war in 1990, the French authorities were fully aware of the risk of ethnic war and genocide in the country. In its efforts to ensure the disintegration of the RPF the French financed and shipped significant volumes of arms to the FAR (McNulty 2000). In addition, Rwanda made clandestine contact with Egypt to negotiate an arms deal, liaising directly with Boutros Boutros-Ghali, then a Foreign Office official in Cairo but later installed as UN Secretary-General, a role that he fulfilled throughout the period of the 1994 genocide. The Governments of Rwanda and Egypt concluded their negotiations in late October, and Habyarimana took receipt of almost $6m of weapons, inclusive of mortars and ammunition, with a French-Government-controlled bank acting as insurer for the funds deposited (Malone 2004).

Having launched Operation Noroît, France was empowered to organise and train members of the FAR and the specially recruited Presidential Guard. The ostensible purpose of Noroît was to protect Europeans, but a clandestine element within it called Panda *Détachement d'assistance militaire et d'instruction* (DAMI) provided direct support to the Rwandan army (Charbonnea 2008: 135). There is also corroborated evidence that the French military of Operation Noroît was responsible for actively training thousands of the Hutu militiamen of the *Interahamwe* and the smaller *Impuzamugambi* who later would become the main perpetrators of the crime of genocide (Interviews, Rwanda, 2006). The French also supplied the FAR with

Panhard armoured cars, heavy artillery and Gazelle helicopters (Interview with Dieu Mucyo, Rwanda, 2005). A former FAR soldier stated that 'in 1990 the French came with the guns and taught us how to use them. The French soldiers went into battle with us, fighting the RPF, but it was only the French that fired the heavy guns' (Interview with Bosco, Rwanda, 2006). Such military intervention by the specialist military forces of Operation Noroît/Panda who arrived in October 1990 was in fact a breach of the Franco-Rwandan agreement of 1975, which clearly specified the French military was only legally permitted to organise and instruct the Rwandese national police. However, in order to put the French on a legal footing with Rwanda, and to enable continued future assistance against their perceived Anglo-Saxon threat from the north, the 1975 Franco-Rwandan agreement was amended on 26 August 1992 to entitle the FAR to French military assistance. Two years after the *de facto* modification caused by the RPF attack of October 1990, this amendment legally permitted the French to continue with their military training of the FAR whilst providing a veil for the clandestine and not-so-legal schooling of the Hutu militiamen who subsequently progressed to being the main groups responsible for large scale massacres in 1994 (Charbonneau 2008: 126).

There is additional evidence that, despite pronouncements that Operation Noroît would not interfere in Rwandan internal affairs, the French influence on Rwandan national defence was not restricted to the physical coaching of firearms training, the art of strangulation and the construction of clubs from wood. Fieldwork evidences that the future *génocidaires* were also provided with ideological indoctrination by the French. Nicholas Bizimungu, a former Rwandan soldier, said, 'The French soldiers would teach us that the Tutsi were our enemies and that we should kill them at any opportunity. The French taught us that if we allowed the Tutsi to return, they would take over our country. They would cause us to perish' (Interview, Rwanda, 2006). Another former Rwandan soldier, Bernardin Uwera, indicated that the French told the FAR, 'your enemy is the Tutsi. As long as they are alive, the Hutu will never be comfortable. Figure out a way of killing them and finishing them' (Interview, Rwanda, 2006). Witnesses and photographic evidence substantiate that French soldiers directly assisted Rwandan army units in civilian areas and indeed an investigation by Human Rights Watch during Rwanda's civil war 'observed French soldiers manning checkpoints ... They were armed with 5.56mm FAMAS automatic rifles, as well as Wasp 58 assault rocket launchers and other infantry support weapons. Like Rwandan army troops, French troops demanded identification from passing civilians' (Human Rights Watch Arms Project 1994: 23).

With the assistance of Operation Noroît, the Rwanda army quickly repulsed the invasion of the RPF in 1990. However, the French military remained visibly present in Rwanda thereafter. When its initial attack was repulsed, the RPF retreated, carrying out a series of guerrilla incursions into Rwanda that were met with rapid retaliatory action by the Rwandan army, ably assisted by the French. Habyarimana's regime reacted strategically, staging indiscriminate attacks on Rwandan civilians and thereafter issuing press releases identifying RPF infiltrators as the culprits for the attacks, which provided the Government with credible grounds for arresting Tutsi civilians suspected of supporting the RPF. The thousands of detainees would be held without charge, often for months, in deplorable conditions. Many were tortured and dozens died.

By the summer of 1992, hard diplomatic negotiations were underway to establish a ceasefire in the ongoing civil war, with a new RPF strike anticipated at any moment. International pressure mounted on Habyarimana to share power. Sanctions were applied or threatened by the international community, including French officials who warned the Rwandan president that they would soon withdraw their troops. Habyarimana knew that without the French presence in his country he would face imminent defeat at the hands of the RPF, so bowing to international pressure, he reluctantly signed the first Arusha protocol. In an effort to move the peace negotiations forward, a US deputy assistant secretary arranged for the RPF and GOR to hold talks in Harare in July 1992. Paris was incensed by the US intervention, which was perceived as an attempt to commandeer French efforts to bring peace in Rwanda, ensuring a prompt reaction from Paris (Wallis 2006).

In April 1993, the Special Rapporteur on Extrajudicial, Summary or Arbitrary Executions of the United Nations Commission on Human Rights warned of acts of genocide in Rwanda against the Tutsi minority, which echoed the conclusions of an international fact-finding mission composed of non-governmental organisations that had visited the country some weeks earlier (Schabas 2000). France maintained a permanent diplomatic mission in Kigali and the embassy was able to keep abreast of the hate propaganda broadcast over the airwaves and printed in newspapers, as well as the persistent massacres committed by some of those who became perpetrators of genocide.

On the arrival of UNAMIR in Rwanda in October 1993, the French military made no effort to conceal its disdain for the mission and its commander, believing they too were encroaching on French territory (Wallis 2006: 69). However, such disdain was not one-sided: one less-than-enthusiastic UN official told the BBC that UNAMIR was merely 'taking in France's dirty linen' (BBC Panorama 1995). Martres confirms that genocide was foreseeable from October 1993 (Assembleé Nationale, Mission d'Information Commune 1998: 281), yet the French administration continues to deny the predictability of the 1994 genocide.

Operation Noroît officially left Rwanda in December 1993, but elements of the French military attachment remained in Rwanda covertly and continued military training up to and throughout the period of the genocide the following year (Interviews with former members of FAR, Rwanda, 2006). The French investigative journalist Saint-Exupéry (1998b) has also established that two

French intelligence officers attached to Operation Noroît remained in Kigali from where they were able to covertly tap into the telephone network, including interception and monitoring of telephone conversation to and from Rwanda's foreign embassies based in Kigali.

'It's in hard times that you know your friends'

For the two years prior to the genocide, Rwanda was Sub-Saharan Africa's third-largest importer of weapons – quite a feat for one of the smallest countries in Africa. McNulty indicates that '[t]he headwaters of the flow of weapons to conflict in the African Great Lakes are to be found in those Western countries with the world's largest arms industries, notably the US, France, UK and Belgium' (2000: 108). As previously mentioned, although not the sole supplier, France delivered military supplies and secure telecommunications equipment to the extremist regime in Rwanda, and this played an integral role in the unfolding tragedy in 1994 (Des Forges 1999: 814). When the intensive massacres of Tutsi and Hutu moderates commenced on the night of 6 April 1994, traditional weapons and farming implements, including machetes, knives and hoes, were the main tools of the militia. Evidence suggests, however, that the Rwandan army and Presidential Guard often turned automatic rifles and grenades on survivors seeking refuge in churches, stadiums, and school buildings, and as such firearms can clearly be viewed as a crucial factor of the Rwandan genocide (Prunier 1995/2002).

Very soon after the genocide started in Rwanda, six French expatriates lost their lives. This resulted in action by the French government, in coordination with other countries of the West, evacuate all European citizens from Rwanda. The operation, codenamed Amaryllis, engaged in Rwanda from 8 to 14 April 1994. Notably, the first family removed from Rwanda by the French was Habyarimana's widow and 30 members of her family who were suspected of being responsible for some of the excesses of violence perpetrated by the government of Rwanda during the preceding civil war. Tutsi members of staff at the French embassy were left in Rwanda by the French, later killed by the Hutu *génocidaires* (Peterson 2001). Those entering the French embassy after the evacuation of its staff found vast quantities of documentation destroyed, thought to contain evidence of French collusion in the Habyarimana regime (Wallis 2006).

However, Amaryllis was not merely an expatriate evacuation. Colonel Luc Marchal, a UN official, testifies that on 9 April 1994, a French military plane attached to Operation Amaryllis, landed at Kigali airport with a full load of military arms, which were unloaded directly to members of FAR before the French soldiers reverted to their role of assisting with the evacuation of Europeans from Rwanda (BBC Panorama 1995).

UNAMIR Commander Dallaire was incensed by the conduct of the French members of Amaryllis, whom he accuses of stealing UN vehicles from the airport and opening fire on several occasions whilst driving them (Callamard 2000). The French commander of Operation Amaryllis does not dispute being in possession of said UN vehicles without permission but justifies their activities, claiming to have masked the UNAMIR signwriting with French flags (Wallis 2006).

Deliveries of arms to FAR from France continued throughout the genocide (McNulty 2000; Peterson 2001). Patrick Kirezi, a former member of the *Interahamwe* testifies that as a French shipment of arms was being unloaded from a French military plane at Goma airport, the French were assuring them, 'You cannot be defeated because we support you. Once we unloaded the planes we were issued with the weapons and boarded onto buses at Goma to be taken to Kigali or some other place' (Interview, Rwanda, 2006).

On 17 May 1994, a UN arms embargo (Resolution 918) mandated a halt to all arms shipments to Rwanda. However, as late as 18 July 1994, arms originating from France were delivered to the genocidal Hutu regime in exile in Zaire under the guise of Operation Turquoise (Saint-Exupéry 1998a). McNulty (2000) argues that the sheer scale of French arms sales to Rwanda in the period immediately preceding the genocide and during the genocide played a conclusive role in sustaining and escalating the violence.[7] The French consul in Goma said these were legitimate shipments that had been ordered and paid for long before the genocide occurred (Peterson 2001).

As a permanent member of the UNSC, the French played a significant role in the decision-making processes of the Council. Interviews with former ambassadors to the UNSC (various locations, 2005–06) clearly evidenced that the French representatives of the UNSC chose not to share the substantial information and intelligence at their disposal, gathered during their three-year engagement in Rwanda. There is no doubt that both the non-permanent and some of the permanent members of the UNSC were kept deliberately uninformed, not least by the then UN Secretary-General, Francophone Boutros Boutros-Ghali, who had facilitated the arms deal between Egypt and Rwanda some four years previously. A declassified cable, forwarded from the UK Mission to the United Nations (UKMIS NY) to the FCO in London and the British High Commission in Kampala, reveals that personnel of UKMIS NY suspected for some time that Boutros-Ghali was not fully presenting all available intelligence and had now received confirmation of same (Document in possession of author).

The French 'resolution'

By the end of May 1994, the RPF had advanced and secured Kigali airport. By controlling most of eastern Rwanda, the RPF had effectively put a halt to the genocide of Tutsi in this area. Human rights organisations, and even the French Foreign Minister Alain Juppé, were by now describing the events in Rwanda as 'genocide', albeit Juppé accused both factions for the slaughter in the country. Indeed, Mitterrand voided suspicions of a double-genocide in Rwanda (Wallis 2006: 187). By mid-June there were few Tutsis left to rescue in Rwanda, as the relentless massacre had all but succeeded in exterminating its targets with the exception of a few scattered pockets of survivors principally in the Bisesero region of Kibuye Province. It was self-evident that the RPF had virtually toppled the Hutu regime.

It was in full knowledge of these conditions that, on 20 June, France put forward a draft resolution to the UNSC for a self-funded 'humanitarian intervention' in Rwanda, codenamed Operation Turquoise. Resolution 929 was authorised by the UNSC on 22 June 1994, providing the French intervention with an aura of authenticity. Operation Turquoise was granted a Chapter VII mandate and described in Resolution 929 as 'a temporary multinational force' to establish secure humanitarian areas by 'all necessary means including the use of force' (UN Doc S/RES/929). The duration of deployment was limited to two months. This development was incredibly frustrating for the UNAMIR Force Commander Dallaire, who had unsuccessfully lobbied the United Nations for some two months to have his Chapter VI mandate upgraded to a Chapter VII operation, which would have permitted the use of force. Dallaire strenuously opposed the UN authorisation of a second UN-mandated mission into the same country, raising concerns about there being two missions in one country with conflicting mandates, 'but ultimately I knew the French were using a humanitarian cloak to intervene in the country' (Interview, London, 2005). The UNSC authorisation of Resolution 929 raised much domestic cynicism in France, with French newspapers printing scathing allegations of their government's blatant complicity in the preparation and implementation of the genocide in Rwanda (Nundy 1994).

When interviewed, one member of the 1994 British Cabinet stated, 'The real blinder the French played was to get Security Council agreement to this [Resolution 929]'. There was in fact distinct apathy within the UNSC to Resolution 929, with five abstentions out of a total of 15 Council members. Few on the UNSC believed that France was motivated solely by humanitarian concerns (Interview with Colin Keating, New York, 2006). The general opinion within the UNSC was that it was virtually unimaginable that France had had 'a crisis of conscience', and much more believable that it was about to use the United Nations's seal of approval as cover to protect French interests in Rwanda and save Hutu *génocidaires* from retribution (Interviews with former members of UKMIS NY, 2006). 'I believed there were other reasons [for the intervention] … any humanitarian consequences of the deployment were purely a by-product', stated another former British Cabinet member.

In addition to the French military, a few hundred troops from Senegal and Chad, and about 40 from the Congo and Niger, supported Operation Turquoise. Dallaire argues that 'this was solely to give it an aura of multilateralism, but it was far from this' (Interview with Dallaire, London, 2005). Prunier argues that what finally pushed President Mitterrand to take action in

Rwanda was South African President Nelson Mandela's declaration of his intention to respond to the Great Lakes crisis when addressing the Tunis meeting of the OAU on 13 June 1994 – a statement viewed by the French president as 'another member of the Anglo-Saxon world who was openly saying that he was about to intervene in French-speaking Rwanda' (Prunier 1995/2002: 281).

The very day after Resolution 929 was passed, the French military arrived in Rwanda, heavily armed with marine mortars, light and heavy helicopters, fighter-bombers, ground attack planes, reconnaissance planes and more than 100 armoured vehicles. Dallaire noted that there were very few trucks and, moreover, those trucks present had no lift capabilities such as would be required for a humanitarian intervention. This confirmed his suspicions that Turquoise was primarily a military intervention despite the stipulation by the UNSC that the intervention was for humanitarian purposes (Interview, London, 2005). It was also noted by Dallaire and members of FAR that many of the French soldiers and commanders of Operation Turquoise had previously been garrisoned in Rwanda with Operation Noroît. A subsequent French Parliamentary Commission report on Rwanda (1999) confirmed that fact, stating that the use of such troops 'without doubt created a source of ambiguity and encouraged mistrust and scepticism'.

Rather than quashing the massacres and drawing a halt to genocide in Rwanda, the arrival of the French troops of Operation Turquoise appeared to buoy the spirits of the near defeated *génocidaires* who felt protected by the arrival of their long-term ally and reinvigorated to complete their task of exterminating the few remaining Tutsi. One current Rwandan government official who survived the genocide witnessed the *Interahamwe* militia responsible for the majority of the atrocities 'giving the French a very warm welcome. There was much shouting and dancing in the street and French tricolours being waved around, and the [French] flags were hung even on the Rwandan Army military vehicles. The killers were shouting "*Vive La France*"' (Interview with Dieu Mucyo, Rwanda, 2005). Despite entering the country with a UN mandate, the French troops did not wear the blue berets of the United Nations. Instead the French government insisted that they wear the green and red berets of the French elite paratroopers and marines – not troops one would normally encounter in a 'humanitarian' role.

Indeed, the arrival of the French military in June 1994 *allowed* the massacre of the Tutsi of Rwanda to continue unchecked for an extra month. Contrary to their humanitarian mandate, witnesses have testified that French soldiers of Operation Turquoise actively killed Tutsis trapped at the *Interahamwe* militia roadblocks. Clementine Gasana, a Tutsi survivor of Kigali stated, 'Yes, the French did genocide and they helped people who did genocide … During the genocide they would help the *Interahamwe* with the roadblocks and check the identity cards to try and catch Tutsi civilians' (Interview, Rwanda, 2006). One ex-FAR soldier who worked alongside members of the

French intervention stated, 'I did not see French soldiers shooting openly but when they captured Tutsi at road blocks they would put them into their trucks and drive them to the barracks ... the people caught on the roadblock were never seen again' (Interview, Rwanda, 2006). According to Didier Gasana, who joined the *Interahamwe* before the start of the genocide, Tutsi prisoners arrested by the French at roadblocks were killed and loaded into trucks by the *Interahamwe*, and the bodies were dumped in Lake Vert. He claims that six French soldiers would provide an escort to the trucks carrying the corpses of the Tutsi detainees (Interview, Rwanda, 2006).

Evidence has also been obtained of soldiers, deployed by Operation Turquoise, torturing persons suspected of being RPF. Interviewees, including a former soldier with the Rwandan army, and a former mayor in Karama Commune, state that they saw the French arresting people during the genocide. 'They tied them up and then beat them badly. They then took them by helicopter to Nyungwe forest and pushed them out of the choppers from the air' (Interviews, Rwanda, 2006). Celestin Mutangana survived being tortured by the French and thrown from one of their helicopters. When interviewed he displayed visible scarring to his body (Rwanda, 2006).

By early July, Rwandan Hutus were fleeing in their thousands across borders into refugee camps within Tanzania and Zaire; the interim government of Rwanda fled into the Safe Humanitarian Zone (SHZ) of Operation Turquoise, where looting was freely taking place under the gaze of the French. A former Rwandan soldier stated when interviewed (Rwanda, 2005) that French soldiers were actively stealing cars, which were subsequently resold in Zaire. France promised the international community that it would arrest the architects of the genocide who had by now fled into the SHZ, however, 'striving ... to keep open the possibility of future power-sharing negotiations, the French actually facilitated the safe passage to Zaire of the Hutu government, the army, and the militias' (Kuperman 2001: 50). This included Colonel Théoneste Bagosora who has since been convicted of crimes of genocide at the ICTR (2008). One British eyewitness stated that 'French soldiers who arrived in Butare on July 1 ... evacuated Bagosora, flying him out on July 2' (Kiley, cited in Des Forges 1999).

Case-study Bisesero: a 'thorn in the side of the *génocidaires*'

An area of great beauty and undulating, rolling hills, Bisesero lies in south-west Rwanda, in the prefecture of Kibuye. Bisesero is 28km from the small town of Kibuye, and the narrow, winding mountainous roads that have to be negotiated to reach the hills of Bisesero ensure slow progress. The mountains rise to 2,400m and are separated by deep valleys; in the higher slopes there are steep forested hillsides dotted with caves. The genocidal massacres of 1994 began at a slightly slower pace in Kibuye prefecture because of its high concentration of Tutsi. When the killings started, thousands of Tutsi from the surrounding communes fled to the Bisesero region where they staged a steadfast resistance against their Hutu attackers. The historical reputation of the residents of Bisesero region as a warrior people attracted other Tutsis seeking protection to the region. During the genocide, the Hutu militia established a base at Gishyita, a 20-minute drive from the Bisesero mountains, giving them easy access to their prey (Interview with former member of *Interahamwe* militia, Rwanda, 2006).

The Tutsi people of Bisesero were poorly armed, as Emmanuel Masozera testifies: 'At the start of the killings we only had a few machetes and clubs, but the killers were armed with guns and grenades. We also had stones to throw that the women had collected. The women were really truly brave. We didn't think it would last long' (Interview, Rwanda, 2005). The Hutu militia would attack during the day and then withdraw in the late afternoon, only to resume their attacks the following day. The resistance fighters of Bisesero would lie in the ground waiting until the Hutu were close before rising to face their attackers in hand-to-hand combat. But they were no competition for the well-armed and well-fed Hutu militia (ibid). Resistance did however continue in Bisesero and eventually the local militia called for reinforcements from the Presidential Guard, the army, and the police to help suppress the remaining resisters. In the words of one survivor, they had become 'a thorn in the side of the *génocidaires*' (Interview, Rwanda, 2005).

The result of this call to arms was described by one defendant at the ICTR who stated that '[a]fter a period of relative calm, on 13 May 1994, thousands of Tutsi (estimated by one witness to number between 15,000 and 40,000) who had sought refuge [at Bisesero] were subjected to a major attack and massacred'. Another witness estimated that only 10,000 of the 40,000–50,000 refugees survived the attack. Other accounts claimed 'there were 5,000–15,000, predominantly Hutu attackers, armed with rifles, grenades, and traditional weapons'.[8]

Survivors of Bisesero indicate that by late June 1994, of the peak number of 65,000 people resisting in Bisesero, about 2,000 remained alive. Witnesses describe these emaciated survivors as suffering from untreated wounds and hiding in caves or within the densely wooded forests (Interviews, Rwanda, 2005). The resisters of Bisesero learned from one of their few working radios that French soldiers had arrived in Kibuye Prefecture with a UN mandate to stop the genocide and thought their prayers had been answered (Interviews, Rwanda, 2005).

Prayers answered? Operation Turquoise enters Kibuye

On arrival, the French established roadblocks and a military post at Gishyita, a location that had been used by thousands of the *Interahamwe* militia as a meeting place for their daily assaults against the Tutsis who were in hiding in the Bisesero mountains. Robert Hakizimana, Jean Inyumba and Fabien Gara, former members of the *Interahamwe*, claim that they manned the roadblocks established by Operation Turquoise alongside the French soldiers and it was a common occurrence for civilians to be killed at the roadblocks, including women and children, in the presence of the French (Interviews, Rwanda, 2005). Another former *Interahamwe* detailed how French soldiers spectated as the local Hutu militia leaders briefed the *Interahamwe* before organising their day's transportation into the 'killing fields' of the Bisesero mountains (ibid). Other former FAR and *Interahamwe* militia claim the French soldiers handed them guns and grenades and they would thereafter move set off up the mountains on foot whilst others were transported in buses, trucks or French jeeps (ibid). Jean Inyumba reveals that once the *génocidaires* left the base at Gishyita, the French used military telescopes to monitor the militia 'working' on the hillsides (Interview, Rwanda, 2006). When the Hutu militia returned to Gishyita each evening from the mountains, those in command would meet with the French soldiers at the military centre to inform them of the events of the day in Bisesero (ibid).

On 26 June, several British journalists arrived in Kibuye and became aware of the plight of the surviving resisters of Bisesero. One of these journalists informed the French soldiers at Gishyita that he was aware of the continuing slaughters at Bisesero and that he intended to forward an article to his editor that evening, detailing how massacres were continuing in the region despite the arrival of Operation Turquoise (Kiley 1994). The following day a former *Interahamwe* and self-confessed killer was approached by French soldiers in Gishyita. When interviewed, he claimed '[t]hey bought me a Primus [beer] and asked me to take them to Bisesero' (Interview, Rwanda, 2006). The French were escorted mid afternoon onto Bisesero hill by some *Interahamwe* militia who travelled in a separate vehicle from the 30 or so French soldiers. Some of the *Interahamwe* were wearing the uniform of the Red Cross. One survivor of Bisesero stated:

> They had three cars, two of them [armoured personnel carriers] of French soldiers and the third car with the militia [*Interahamwe*] but it stopped a short distance away. We said 'lets go there' when the cars had separated and stopped. 'If they kill us they kill us'. Not long before they came, the *Interahamwe* had killed some of our people and they [the bodies] were near me. Three were dead but two were still hot. We went and picked them and took them to the French cars. One had been shot and two were dead by machetes. I talked to the French soldiers through the window of the car [APC] and asked what help they could be to us. They stayed in their cars. They said they needed to know how many of us were here and said to bring everyone down out of the forests and onto the road.
>
> (Interview, Rwanda, 2005)

Another witness who survived the massacres at Bisesero told the author that, because they were desperate, they were prepared to take a risk despite seeing that the French had arrived accompanied by *Interahamwe* militia, some of whom they recognised as being responsible for massacres at Bisesero over the previous weeks. They believed they would be safe from the militia as there were French helicopters circling above. By using loudspeakers to hail people, 'the French were instrumental in talking the people out of their places of hiding' (Interview, Rwanda, 2005).

Bosco Isibo stated:

> The French waited till we had done what they had asked and we were all out of hiding and gathered together on the road. They had started to look anxious. They just said, 'we cannot help you just now'. They said they didn't have lorries and would have to leave but promised they would come back soon. The French soldiers took the guns we had taken from the killers. We had eighteen guns but it did not matter because we had no ammunition and did not know how to work them. They must have thought we would be able to shoot our killers.
>
> (Interview, Rwanda, 2005)

It was the feeling of the survivors of Bisesero that the convoy of French troops seemed quite disinterested when they arrived in the area. Charles Uwinkidi claims that, until they arrived in Bisesero, the French considered the Hutu to be the victims of genocide and not the Tutsi; however, after seeing the bodies of Tutsi recently slaughtered by the *Interahamwe*, some of the soldiers realised that it was the Hutu that were the perpetrators of genocide (ibid). On his return to Kibuye, one of the *Interahamwe* militia, a former teacher who had escorted the French onto the Bisesero Mountains, informed his militia leaders of the numbers and location of the remaining surviving Tutsi on the hillsides, and plans were made to destroy the last of the resisters of the region. He claims that 'the French had no plans to save any of these Tutsi, our aims were the same – to kill the Tutsi. The French supported the mission of the Hutu' (Interview with Gusto, Rwanda, 2006). Only hours after the arrival of the French at Bisesero, the surviving Tutsis faced some of the worst genocidal attacks to date.

Diego, the French officer in charge of the convoy that assembled the survivors of Bisesero was sickened by the duplicity of his military superiors and the reality that the true victims of genocide in the Bisesero mountains were the Tutsi he had just met, and not the Hutu as they had been briefed. On his return to base that evening, he filed a report on his afternoon findings and consulted his superiors within Operation Turquoise for direction. He fully expected to be returning to Bisesero at first light to evacuate those who were clearly in mortal danger. He was prevented from taking such action by the direct orders of his superior officers who were unperturbed at his concerns over the imminent danger to the hundreds of Tutsi he had seen on the hills (Saint-Exupéry 2004: 87). Diego made numerous phone calls to Paris and was frustrated by the resistance of higher military and government officials, 'who, despite Turquoise's alleged humanitarian mandate, seemed inclined to resist intervention' (Wallis 2006: 152). The French officer took the decision to disobey the orders of his commanders, and, in the company of the French journalist Patrick de Saint-Exupéry, Diego departed camp in convoy with his troops to return to Bisesero and attempt to evacuate the remaining survivors. His efforts were almost immediately thwarted by the arrival of the head of the special elite forces attached to Operation Turquoise, himself a veteran of Operation Noroît, who landed his helicopter on the road in front of the convoy thereby preventing passage (Saint-Exupéry 2004: 83–4). It was two days later on 30 June that Diego, accompanied by the same journalist and troops, once again disobeyed direct orders and returned to Bisesero where they found over one thousand people massacred since their initial visit to the area some three days previously. Under pressure because of the presence of the media, their superior officers at base camp relented and steps were taken to rescue the desperate survivors who were barely alive (ibid: 89). Had the French acted in a manner appropriate to their mandate, many more of the people would have survived at Bisesero on 27 June 1994.

The actual number of Tutsi killed in Bisesero between 9 April and 30 June is uncertain. African Rights (1998) estimate that some 50,000 people were killed at Bisesero; survivors interviewed by the author reported as many as 75,000 killed. Perhaps the negligence of Operation Turquoise at Bisesero is an extreme example, and yet indicative of the approach of a section of the upper echelons in the French government.

It would be remiss to only allude to negative aspects of Turquoise; one must not ignore the humanitarian achievements of the operation. Several studies have estimated the number of Rwandans saved by the French. Prunier (1995/2002) has estimated that between 13,000–14,000 people were saved during the mission, while Adelman and Suhrke (1996) estimate 10,000–15,000. Des Forges (1999) has also acknowledged that the French saved people in Rwanda, estimating the number of lives saved at around 17,000. However, she highlights with some contempt that this somewhat minor achievement was the best efforts of a force of the best-equipped elite paratroopers, when 'UNAMIR, with its barely 500 men, poorly armed and equipped, protected at one time nearly twice that number' (ibid: 689).

Operation Turquoise provides many grounds for criticism. The stated humanitarian aims and objectives of the mission were barely fulfilled. Such was the need to remain credible in the eyes of France's African allies, many of whom were longstanding dictators and tyrants, that much of Turquoise's work was in reality directed towards preventing an RPF victory.

A confidential newsletter, reputed to originate in French Government circles, showed the cynical disregard with which some of the French military and political establishment viewed the on going genocide. Titled 'Considerable political and geostrategic interests are hidden behind the Rwandese heap of corpses', it argues that Rwanda was a key to the region and could not be 'lost' to Anglophone influences. The newsletter ended as follows:

> the region cannot be left in the hand of an English-speaking strongman completely aligned to American views and interests. That is why, since 1990, France has supported the late President Juvénal Habyarimana in order to fight the RPF. It did not work out so now the only choice left to us is to put back in the saddle the Zairian President Mobutu Sese Seko, the one man capable of standing up to Museveni.
>
> (Prunier 1995/2002: 278–9)

Post-genocide relations in Rwanda

The military victory of the RPF and the fall of Kigali on 4 July 1994 was viewed by France as the first time a Francophone African country had fallen, not just to a rebel force, but one with Anglo-Saxon influence. Some in the French administration accurately foresaw the fall of the Hutu-dominated regime of Rwanda as the beginning of a series of regional 'dominoes', that might eventually lead to Anglo-Saxon domination of large portions of the Great Lakes region and would prove detrimental to France and *la Francophonie* (Glaser and Smith 1994).

On 6 July 1994, Turquoise accepted that 'Kagame had won the war … An uneasy peace came into effect between the two sides with the RPF tolerating the SHZ, while the French in turn restrained the more belligerent members of their staff who wanted a crack at Kagame's men' (Wallis 2006: 160). France's actions after the genocide mirrored the acerbity it felt in the midst of an RPF defeat of the Hutu regime in Rwanda. French representatives stormed out of conferences when the president of the government of national unity stood up, France denied aid to Rwanda, and did its utmost to thwart EU assistance to the country.

One senior French military officer was heard to proclaim 'the worst is yet to come. Those bastards will go all the way to Kinshasa now. And how in God's name am I going to explain to our friends [Francophone heads of state] that we have let down one of our own' (Prunier 1995/2002: 337n). The French Government took consolation in its *erroneous* assumption that the RPF would be short-term rulers of Rwanda, hypothesising that by facilitating the escape of its former Rwandan allies, it would survive to fight another day and bring pressure to bear on the RPF. The devastating consequences of the French policy are illuminated by the subsequent wars in the DRC and the daily atrocities that continue in eastern DRC to this day.

Mitterrand – 'Our responsibility is none'

Despite overwhelming evidence to the contrary, the French Government still insists that it bears no responsibility for the genocide in Rwanda. In an interview of September 1994 published in *Le Figaro,* then-President Mitterrand stated, 'Our responsibility is none' (cited in Kroslak 2007: 271).

In 1998, as a result of pressure from civil society, non-governmental organisations and reporters (most notably Patrick de Saint-Exupéry, who raised serious questions about the depth and extent of French support for the Habyarimana dictatorship and genocidal regime in Rwanda from 1990 until the end of the genocide in 1994), the French Parliamentary Commission on Rwanda was instructed to investigate French policy towards Rwanda. In the final report (1998), the Commission skilfully exonerated France from any responsibility in the Rwandan genocide. The report concluded that the French Parliamentary Committee do not support the 'unacceptable accusation' that France was complicit in the genocide.

Though French troops did compile their own lists of people accused of taking part in the killing, these were never given to the United Nations or the ICTR. Internal reports from the French military indicate that French soldiers believe their superiors tricked them, having been led to believe that it was the Hutus of Rwanda who were the victims of genocide. Indeed, many French soldiers complained to journalists on location at Kibuye during Operation Turquoise that they had been 'duped' by their own government (McGreal 2007). One French sergeant watching over a group of machete-scarred, emaciated Tutsi survivors in early July 1994, told a journalist 'we have been deceived ... this is not what we were led to believe. We were told that Tutsis were killing Hutus. We thought the Hutus were the good guys and the victims' (Gourevitch 1998: 160). The identity of the true victims of genocide was successfully distorted with one French report even suggesting that the Tutsi were 'committing collective suicide' (Hintjens 1999: 274). The Tutsi diaspora who made up the RPF were identified by the French as Ugandan Anglophones and described in exceedingly inflammatory and derogatory terminology as '*Khmer Noir*' (Black Khmers) in reference to the genocide and killing fields of Cambodia (Kroslak 2007); furthermore, no distinction was made between the Tutsi of Rwanda and the Tutsi diaspora of the RPF. In a BBC *Panorama* broadcast, French politicians and military commanders dismissed the RPF as a group of 'terrorists and killers' (1995).

Such representations by the French commanders and Hutu officials ensured that the French soldiers stood by as the governor of Kibuye led militia attacks into the hills of Bisesero to exterminate the small pocket of remaining Tutsi survivors (McGreal 2007). The realisation of having been deceived by its own government about the role of the *Interahamwe* in genocide, resulted in some bitterness within the French army. One internal army document speaks of 'soldiers who cracked, not because of the corpses and violence and hunting down victims ... but because of a sense of guilt' (Saint-Exupéry, cited in Pfaff 1998). One French commander reported being 'misinformed about what was happening in front of his eyes and later humiliated at what he had been drawn into by the politicians in Paris' (McGreal 2007).

The current GOR has made repeated accusations against France in relation to the genocide. In April 2005, Article 2 of the Organic Law of Rwanda established a 'Commission of Enquiry to Establish the Role of France in the Genocide of 1994' headed by the former Chief Prosecutor General and Minister of Justice, Jean de Dieu Mucyo and referred to generally as the Mucyo Commission. This was a domestic tribunal made up of a seven-member panel of historians, legal experts and a senior military officer of the former Rwandan army. The Mucyo Commission gathered evidence at hearings throughout a seven-day period in October 2006 and a further seven-day period in December 2006, the aim being to make formal recommendations to the GOR on whether or not to take legal action against France for genocide-related damages at the ICJ. The three-volume, 337-page report was released on 5 August 2008. The Mucyo Commission report names former French President Mitterand, his son Jean-Christophe Mitterand and several members of his cabinet as well as senior military officials among those who should be held responsible for the slaughter of over a million people in 1994.

In addition, the report identifies 20 French military and 13 political figures who, the Mucyo Commission argues, have a solid criminal case to answer. Despite the fact that France considers itself the birthplace of human rights, Paris has refused to permit its soldiers to testify before any court with regards to the genocide in Rwanda.

It must be acknowledged that November 2006 witnessed a bitter diplomatic dispute between Kigali and Paris after the French Judge Jean-Louis Bruguiere called for Rwandan President Paul Kagame to be brought before an international criminal tribunal accused of being responsible for the death of President Juvénal Habyarimana when his plane was attacked by a surface to air missile in 1994. France has also made allegations that the RPF committed human rights abuses and massacres. Bruguiere is seeking to bring Kagame and eight other high-ranking Rwandan officials before a UN tribunal, and to this end issued arrest warrants in November 2006 to facilitate such a prosecution (Africa Research Bulletin 2006).

French policy in Africa post-genocide

Despite formidable human rights abuses by its 'client' African governments, France has, until recently, continued to support dictators and regimes that have abusive and murderous policies towards their own people. The longevity and dynamism of such policies are disturbing, surviving the presidencies of de Gaulle, Pompidou, Giscard d'Estaing, Mitterrand and Chirac, and enduring changing times, values and world politics. With colonisation and 50 years of influence in Africa, a network developed between French and African elites termed *la Françafrique.* Speaking in 1996, a diplomat in the Ivory Coast summed up the equation: 'you could talk about the French presence [in Africa] for hours and hours but it comes down to two things – prestige and business' (French 1996). French policy-making is developed within this special network consisting of politicians, state officials, military officers, heads of oil and weapons firms, and members of the African elite. France's support for numerous dictators, coups and rebellions during the Cold War years can be ascribed to its attachment to *la Françafrique.*

The election of Nicolas Sarkozy to the French Presidency in May 2007 has seen some changes in the country's relationship with Africa and intimations of the demise of corrupt networks with its former African colonies. However, Taylor argues that 'as new actors emerge in Africa, such as China and India, the increased competition of resources and influence may well spur Sarkozy to pursue engagement with Africa – albeit of a different nature than that typified by the discredited concept of *la Françafrique*' (2010: 67).

Conclusion

Genocide does not occur without ideological preparation and practical, logistical and strategic preparation. From 1990 onwards, France performed an integral role in the architecture of the Rwandan genocide. France colluded and conspired with the genocidal Hutu regime, supplying arms and military equipment, military training and dissemination of racialised ideologies to the FAR and Hutu militia organisations.

Once the genocide in Rwanda commenced in April 1994, France knowingly persisted in its collusive, participatory role by continuing to deliver arms and military training to the *génocidaires* throughout the period of Operation Turquoise in breach of a UN arms embargo. The ICTY has clearly indicated that any assistance in genocide constitutes sufficient participation to meet the terms of complicity as defined by the UNGC, and as such it is arguable that the knowing participatory role played by the French, throughout the period of the Rwandan genocide, can be construed as complicity in genocide. Despite having knowledge of the daily suffering of the Tutsi people on the hills of Bisesero, the French soldiers arrived there accompanied by militia, and unequipped to rescue the desperate survivors. These soldiers then left the area, knowing that the wounded and starving Tutsi were in mortal danger, and having learned that the Tutsi were in fact the true victims of genocide, not the perpetrators as they had been led to believe by their leaders.

Exploring France's political and military relationship with Rwanda from 1990 and throughout the period of the genocide of 1994, highlights the emergence of their complicity in genocide as a global elite bystander, revealing with special clarity that the French Government overtly violated international law for political and economic advantage in central Africa. The conduct of the French military at Gishyita is clearly definable as complicity and clearly indicates that power interests rather than humanitarian concern guided the French 'humanitarian' intervention in Rwanda, for which there is a potential for prosecution in terms of the concept of state crime.

Chapter 6

Britain, Uganda and the RPF

Throughout the 17 years since the genocide in Rwanda, the British Government of 1994 has repeatedly excused its decisions and actions in respect of its policy towards Rwanda, claiming to have had no prior interest in the country and no access to intelligence or information. Members of John Major's 1994 Government claim to have been 'uninformed', 'unsighted' and lacking in any semblance of reliable or relevant information about events in the country. However, as this chapter will evidence, this was not in fact the case. Critical to our understanding of the role of the British Government in the Rwandan genocide are the complex events of several years immediately before the genocide, namely from 1990 until early 1994. An exploration of the data available to the British Government during this period of time indicates that its members were in possession of a wealth of detailed, reliable and relevant intelligence, both before and during the Rwandan genocide, which would have allowed them a clear perspective on the unfolding situation in the country. The data explored includes information and intelligence from both official and unofficial sources; official communications and directions between the FCO, the British Embassies of Kinshasa, Kampala and Dar Es Salaam, UKMIS NY, Washington and Cabinet ministers; and interviews undertaken with elite informants from various nations.[1]

Before the genocide in Rwanda in 1994, the United Kingdom did not have a permanent diplomatic mission in either Rwanda or Burundi, although a British Honorary Consul, Tony Wood, was resident in Rwanda throughout the early 1990s.[2] Britain's lack of diplomatic capacity in Rwanda reflects the fact that the United Kingdom had no direct political or financial interests in the country. However, the same is not true of the two countries sharing borders with Rwanda, namely Uganda and the DRC (then Zaire), both of which, unlike Rwanda, were rich in raw materials and had governments that were sympathetic to foreign investment. Britain maintained a strong relationship with President Yoweri Museveni of Uganda, nurtured since his rise to power in 1986. Britain also maintained substantial business interests in Uganda and the DRC. Before 1993, the British Government handled diplomatic issues and maintained foreign relations with Rwanda and Burundi in a variety of *ad hoc* ways. Historically, the British diplomatic offices in Kinshasa and Dar Es Salaam had administered Rwanda and Burundi respectively, but both countries subsequently fell under the administration of Kinshasa. This arrangement changed once again in 1993, when the British High Commissioner of Uganda assumed roving responsibility for diplomacy as a non-resident ambassador in Rwanda. No explanation is available for this policy change, but one can assume that the Uganda-based RPF's influential role on Rwandan politics since 1990 would have been a pivotal factor.

By 1988, it was an open secret in Uganda and Rwanda that Tutsi members of the Ugandan army were planning an invasion of Rwanda (Waugh 2004). Britain supported both the formation of the RPF and its objectives, and from early 1990 onwards, British intelligence services developed a first-rate rapport with the commanders of the guerilla RPF who 'had an excellent and very strong intelligence machine inside Rwanda' (Interview with former British diplomat, 2006). From their base in Uganda, the RPF kept British intelligence abreast of developments within Rwanda. According to a former British official, Kampala, it appeared to many that both the Government of Uganda and the RPF were the cat's paw of the British Government, with the RPF being groomed to overthrow the Francophone Government of Juvénal Habyarimana in Rwanda (Interview, 2006). Military training of the guerrilla RPF in preparation for their incursions into Rwanda was provided by British forces at its military base in Jinja, Uganda (Destexhe 1995) as well as by the US military.

By August 1990 the RPF had started to prepare a full scale invasion of Rwanda, despite the GOR having taken several significant political steps in an effort to avert the RPF invasion. This included the facilitation of the repatriation of the Tutsi refugees from Uganda as demanded by the RPF, with the initial phase scheduled for November 1990. Uganda–Rwanda negotiations on the rights of refugees to claim Rwandan nationality had reached 'an advanced stage' (Mamdani 2001: 159) when the RPF attacked in October 1990. It was only three days prior to the attack that Habyarimana had announced at the UN General Assembly in New York, key concessions to refugees. However, the RPF chose not to allow the validity of Habyarimana's initiatives to be confirmed. It is ironic that the incursion should happen at a time of internal reform as opposed to repression in Rwanda, during a period when President Habyarimana was making efforts to appease the rebel forces.

Britain's SIS was actively engaged in Uganda and was in communication with the RPF, from whom it collated intelligence on the Rwandan government. The relationship between SIS and the RPF ensured the SIS was fully cognizant of the objectives of the RPF and its ability 'to take Kigali pretty much at will'.[3] Because of the level of engagement of both British and American military and intelligence services in Uganda, and their contact with the commanders of the RPF, it is inconceivable that the order for the October 1990 RPF invasion of Rwanda was given without their knowledge, approval and active assistance. Such claims have been forwarded in written submissions to the ICTR by Africa Direct (Chossudovsky 2005).

When the RPF mounted its offensive into Rwanda from southern Uganda on 1 October 1990, the ensuing developments were reported fastidiously to the FCO in London.[4] Throughout October 1990, reports were forwarded daily from the British diplomatic offices in Kampala and Kinshasa to London, giving detailed updates about the incursion, which 'the Ugandan government has made strenuous attempts to distance itself from'.[5] Further telexes advised London of mounting suspicions, both in Rwanda and Uganda, of 'connivance at senior levels in the preparations for the incursion into Rwanda by … the Rwandan Patriotic Front … and Ugandan collusion'.[6] One declassified confidential document dated 4 October from Kampala to London states that some embassies in Kigali 'have agreed to recommend to capitals that there should be a community demarche in Kampala quote seeking to bring the Ugandans to their senses unquote'.[7] The identity of the informant and embassies involved in the proposed community demarche have been deleted from the released documentation. The British High Commissioner in Kampala continues the telex with his opinion that 'such a demarche would be both premature and counter-productive. It … could only damage our interests here'.[8] The FCO accepted the counsel of its High Commissioner in Uganda, and the United Kingdom did not participate in a demarche to Uganda in protestation at the Ugandan Government's ongoing support of the rebel RPF and its attack on Rwanda.

Conspicuous by its absence is the declassification by the FCO of any communications documenting the activities of the GOR during the 1990s that would support the British Government's decision to militarily and ideologically back the Uganda-based rebel guerrilla force of the RPF in its civil war against the elected Government of Juvénal Habyarima of Rwanda.

Almost two weeks after the initial attack RPF on Rwanda, communications from Kampala to London provided intelligence of a meeting held by the Rwandan foreign minister with the resident ambassadors in Kigali, 'at which he claimed that the GOU (government of Uganda) was now actively colluding with the rebels (RPF) … there was anecdotal evidence [presented] to indicate that individuals in senior positions [of the Government of Uganda] … were conniving in attempts to help the rebel cause with supplies'.[9]

SIS operatives continued to play a supporting role in Uganda, liaising with the RPF rebel organisation. On 1 November 1990, a British diplomat in Uganda held a 'further meeting' with a British intelligence operator who had 'met quote senior rebel leaders unquote on 31 October for 3 hours'. This 'classified source' appraised the British diplomat on the current state of the rebel RPF and the conflict in Rwanda, information that was forwarded same day to London by telex.[10]

The following two months witnessed periods of intense fighting followed by extended periods of calm. Then, on 23 January 1991, the British embassy in Kinshasa reported to the FCO in London that the RPF had succeeded in capturing the town of Ruhengeri in northern Rwanda following a dawn raid. London was advised that 'the RPF have shown that they have access to the resources necessary to hit the GOR in important areas. RPF claims to be able to take Kigali pretty much at will can by no means be discounted'.[11] The following day Kampala sent a telex containing similar intelligence to London whereupon receipt a member of FCO staff handwrote on the telex 'this confirms a report from Tony Wood in Kigali which I received yesterday'.[12] This confirms that the British Government was in receipt of multiple sources of information and intelligence, thereby permitting some degree of triangulation.

Further information of the ongoing conflict in Rwanda was also made available to London by the British Embassy in Dar Es Salaam. Peace negotiations at Arusha were initiated in an effort to bring the civil war in Rwanda to an end; these intense meetings were held monthly and the detailed minutes forwarded in full to the FCO in London throughout 1992 and the first few months of 1993.[13] Some of these telexes from the High Commission in Dar Es Salam reporting on the Arusha Peace Process are labelled as 'priority', whilst others are 'routine' or 'immediate'.

Warnings of impending tragedy, or crying wolf?

> NGOs are more reliable because nobody is trying to lobby them or trying to bring them into the process but they witness because they're going round helping in various parts of the country, they actually witness it first hand what is happening.
>
> (Interview with senior member of British Government 1994, London, 2006)

It was January 1993 when Oxfam became 'increasingly fearful of where developments in Rwanda may be heading, and raised its concerns with officials in the British Foreign Office, and with the Secretary of State of the Foreign and Commonwealth Office, Douglas Hurd'.[14] Just a few weeks later, Sir Edward Clay commenced his post as British High Commissioner in Uganda, which included the role of non-resident ambassador to Rwanda. Prior to his departure, Clay was given instructions by the FCO that were recalled by him as:

> We [the British Government] know almost nothing about them [Rwandans] and care less, but you can go there to cover it and we want you to cover it because the main angle for us is the role of the Ugandans as the home of the Rwandans in exile, their supposed or alleged role in supporting

> the RPF and more distantly the repercussions that this little situation in central Africa and their relationship with the French. … Just remember that our relations with Paris will always matter more than our relations with Uganda.
>
> (Interview, London, 2006)

Throughout the first three months of 1993, staff at the British High Commission in Kampala continued to receive warnings from the RPF, albeit somewhat vague in detail, of some catastrophe that was about to occur in Rwanda. There was some suspicion within the British High Commission that the RPF was endeavouring to manipulate the British by crying wolf, 'as was their wanton habit'.[15] The French Government also received warnings of an impending tragedy and, in March 1993, the possibility of some catastrophe unfolding in Rwanda was raised as a topic of discussion within the UNSC, with the French ambassador suggesting the creation of a UN peacekeeping mission for Rwanda (Interview with former UNSC Ambassador, London, 2006). This suggestion was not well received within the UNSC. Some two months later, in May 1993, the Secretary-General, in a report to the UNSC, recommended the creation of a UN observer mission for the Rwanda–Uganda border and as a result, on 22 June 1993, the Security Council adopted Resolution 846 creating the United Nations Observer Mission Uganda–Rwanda (UNOMUR). This mission was deployed on the Ugandan side of the border with a mandate to monitor the border that separated the rebel guerrilla army of the RPF from Rwanda:

> to verify that no military assistance reaches Rwanda, focus being put primarily in this regard on transit or transport, by roads or tracks which could accommodate vehicles, of lethal weapons and ammunition across the border, as well as any other material which could be of military use.
>
> (UN Doc S/1994/846)

In the meantime, peace talks continued in Tanzania, and on 4 August 1993 London received word that 'the long-negotiated peace accord between the government of Rwanda and the Rwandan Patriotic Front was finally signed, amid much rejoicing and considerable relief' (Cable forwarded from Dar es salaam to London 5 August 1993). Shortly thereafter General Dallaire arrived in Kigali, his mission to evaluate the possible role of UN international peacekeepers in the country; in September 1993 the UN Secretary-General recommended to the UNSC the measures that would become Resolution 872 on 5 October 1993 and the establishment of UNAMIR.

The situation within Rwanda was troubling one member of the British Cabinet who recalls being in discussion with the then Foreign Secretary, Lord Hurd and:

> ... getting very cross because we couldn't do more in the UN [Security Council]. This was in the October/November 1993, and it was partly because it was a tiny country, very few people had experience of it. Edward Clay was saying how worried he was, Dallaire found a back route to me, and you know the people who were on the ground were very frightened too.
>
> (Interview, London, 2006)

By December 1993, London was aware that tensions were visible in Rwanda with Government radio stations airing increasingly virulent propaganda against the Tutsi of Rwanda. It became quite clear to some members of the British Government and the United Nations that the Arusha Peace Accords were unsustainable (Interviews, London, 2006). One Cabinet member described them during an interview as 'window dressing' and not being representative of the real situation on the ground (ibid). Within the first few weeks of January 1994, the British High Commission in Kampala informed London that the French Ambassador in Kampala was 'sounding some really deathly warnings ... It was he who spoke first of the use of the term 'cockroach' on *Radio Mille Les Collines*.[16] The French Ambassador to Uganda was also:

> attacking the role of the RPF, claiming that they were bringing about a situation in which there was such tension that it might lead to the contemplation of terrible things; and secondly, the President of Uganda's governments interference by supporting the RPF and alleging that they were actually, you know, fuelling them and supplying them and all that; and thirdly, attacking us (the British Government) because they saw that the Ugandan Government was a cat's paw of the British Government.
>
> (Interview with former British diplomat, London, 2006)

When interviewed (London, 2005), General Dallaire indicated that throughout the first three months of 1994 he visited the foreign embassies in Kigali and warned them of an impending atrocity that was liable to result in many deaths. It is therefore inexplicable why, in the last week of February 1994, when Sir Edward Clay arrived in Rwanda as the non-resident British Ambassador and visited each of the city's embassies in turn, that 'none of his diplomatic colleagues told him anything' (interview with Lynda Chalker,[17] London, 2006). Dallaire met Clay personally during this visit to Rwanda, but did not inform him of his own concerns of an impending atrocity, which Dallaire claimed to have shared with the representatives of the permanent embassies in Rwanda. That no intelligence was shared with Ambassador Clay has been confirmed in interviews with Dallaire, Clay and other diplomats, notably however, Clay advised London that Tony Wood had fled Rwanda in fear of his life (Cable forwarded from Kampala to London, 1 March 1994).

A member of staff from the FCO during this period of time states, 'I don't know why they [Dallaire and foreign Embassies in Kigali] didn't talk to him [Clay]. Either they didn't believe it or they had vested interests' (Interview, London, 2006). During a speech on 22 January 2002, Peter Hain MP, then Minister of State for Foreign Affairs, stated that during February and March 1994, 'General Dallaire, as commander of UNAMIR, found his warnings of impending calamity discounted and disregarded by his superiors in the governments – including that … of the United Kingdom – to which they were reported'. It was General Dallaire himself who informed Hain that his situation reports (sitreps) were being forwarded to United Kingdom intelligence. When interviewed (London, 2005), Dallaire could provide no reason why his sitreps were shared with British intelligence but not the British High Commissioner with roving responsibility for the country concerned.

Britain's role in the UNSC

The British Government is of course one of the five permanent members of the UNSC with a permanent mission in New York. Britain is also a signatory to the UNGC, which imposes a positive obligation to act to prevent genocide globally. In 1994, the most senior British delegate to UKMIS NY was Lord David Hannay.

On 5 April 1994, one day before the assassination of President Habyarimana, the UNSC passed Resolution 909, extending the mandate of UNAMIR until 29 July 1994 with a six-week review on the understanding that progress be made in establishing the transitional institutions provided for by the Arusha Peace Agreement between the GOR and the RPF.

On the day following the death of the Presidents of Rwanda and Burundi, British Ambassador Hannay approved the release of a UNSC Presidential Statement (S/PRST/16) in response to the assassination, which reaffirmed the UNSC's commitment to the Arusha Peace Agreement, and urged all parties to implement it fully. Hannay's position on this matter was official rather than ministerial – in other words, it was on the instructions of London. On the same day, 7 April, the British High Commissioner to Uganda relayed various options to the FCO for what he supposed was the political direction that Rwanda must now face (Cable forwarded from Kampala to London). The FCO in London responded to Clay's telex within four hours of receipt – less than 24 hours after the death of President Habyarimana – stating:

> Agree you should speak to Museveni. … You could point out that the RPF have an important opportunity to participate in power-sharing if they play their cards carefully and constructively. We agree that it should be possible to get these points across without suggesting that we hold Uganda in any way responsible for the RPF or events in Kigali.
>
> (Cable, London to Kampala, 7 April 1994)

This certainly suggests that the British Government was aware of Museveni's instrumental role in the RPF and Rwanda's civil war. The telex from the FCO in London continues, 'Given the uncertainty surrounding the crash, we are for the moment avoiding attributing responsibility to any group' (ibid).

Washington had advised London by telex of the death of the Presidents of Rwanda and Burundi late on the evening of 6 April. The report from Washington concluded that it was 'anyone's guess who was responsible for shooting down the plane' (Cable, Washington to London, 6 April 1994). On the following day, the President of the UNSC, Colin Keating, issued a written statement indicating 'there has been considerable loss of lives, including the deaths of Government leaders, many civilians and at least ten Belgian peacekeepers as well as the reported kidnapping of others' (UN Doc S/PRST/1994/16). Also on 7 April 1994, the British High Commissioner in Kampala sent a telex to FCO London, stating:

> we have spoken to our Honorary Consul [who had since returned to the country], and another informant by the name of Kanyarushoke … both speak of there having been some prolonged periods of shooting. But Kanyarushoke believes this was the Presidential Guards reacting hysterically and firing wildly in the air, rather than to kill.
>
> (Cable, Kampala to London 7 April 1994)

Clay concluded his telex to London by commenting on the political power vacuum in Kigali created by the assassination, concluding that 'Rwanda is in a very dangerous condition' (ibid); it is an accepted fact that the assassination of President Habyarimana triggered genocide in Rwanda.

Declassified documentation reveals that the assassination of President Habyarimana was perceived in British diplomatic circles as something of a positive development in terms of Rwandan politics (Cable, Kampala to London, 9 April 1994). When interviewed, one British Government minister stated that 'the 6th of April 94, in a way, was not a shock at all' (London, 2006). Less than one week after the assassination, the FCO made its High Commissioner in Kampala aware of a statement issued the previous day by the Presidency of the European Union stating that 'the European Union … wants an international commission of inquiry to investigate fully the causes of the destruction of the Presidential aircraft' (Cable, London to Kampala, 13 April 1994). Some 18 years later, no such international commission of inquiry has yet been initiated.

Seven days after the start of the genocide, the British High Commissioner to Uganda held a meeting with the RPF Vice-President Patrick Mazimhaka, affording him the opportunity to put forth his views on the withdrawal of UNAMIR from Rwanda, a subject to be discussed at the following week's meeting of the UNSC in New York. In his reporting of this meeting, Clay informed London that 'the RPF could take care of the current disorder [in Rwanda] and should be left to do so' (Cable, Kampala to London, 13 April 1994). Mazimhaka joined in the regular meeting with all EU Heads of Mission in Kampala, where he advised the congregation that he 'believed the regime [former Government of Rwanda] had a long-laid contingency plan to kill the opposition if really forced into a corner, but they [the RPF] had not expected the degree of brutality employed' (ibid).

The RPF representative was also asked for his thoughts regarding the withdrawal of UNAMIR from Rwanda. His advice was that 'UNAMIR should remain at least until the RPF and the remnants of the government side had seen what help UNAMIR could give them in the new situation. It would not however be necessary to enhance UNAMIR's capacity to intervene: the RPF could take care of the current disorder and should be left to do so' (ibid). Sir Edward Clay advised London that:

> The RPF is acquiring the demeanour of a government in waiting, being pushed by events to assume responsibilities beyond its expectations. Museveni would not fault this approach. *Their claim that only they are in a position to stop the massacres is plausible.* The most dangerous moment for the RPF will indeed arise if the Rwandan population set about each other, perhaps provoked by the army and/or fear of the RPF as a Tutsi force, posing a security problem beyond their power to solve. The RPF seem to see some value in UNAMIR, at least for the time being. It would be premature to change the force's character or mandate until the RPF have attained their military objectives and we can see more clearly what the UN can do to assist in normalising the conditions of life, bringing relief and perhaps facilitating contacts between the RPF and the other parties. [original emphasis]
>
> (ibid)

A few days later, Oxfam launched a 'Victims of Rwanda Emergency' appeal, stating 'the level of violence has shocked everyone' (copy of press release in possession of author). This was followed on 19 April with a further Oxfam press release announcing the arrival in Burundi of two Oxfam Emergency Department members to assess the conditions on the Rwanda–Burundi border (ibid). Oxfam highlighted that 'fighting and killing continues inside Rwanda' and 'Oxfam is extremely concerned about the safety of its 18 local staff in Rwanda, and about the safety of civilians there generally' (ibid). On this same date, Kenneth Roth, Director of Human Rights Watch wrote to the President of the UNSC pointing out that the ongoing atrocities in Rwanda constituted the crime of genocide and urged the five permanent members to fulfil their duty under the UNGC to stop the killings and punish the perpetrators (Robertson 2002: 77).

It must be noted that a telex from the UKMIS NY made London aware of evidence that the UN Secretariat were not forwarding all details of the

UNAMIR Force Commander's 'sitreps' to the UNSC, thereby restricting its ability to make the best judgments on the unfolding situation (Cable UKMIS NY to London, 17 April 1994).

The UNSC adjusts UNAMIR's mandate

It was in this climate that the UN Secretary-General issued the 'Report of the Secretary-General on the United Nation Assistance Mission for Rwanda' dated 20 April 1994 (UN Doc S/1994/470). It advised the UNSC of the deteriorating state of Rwanda and the possible loss of tens of thousands of lives. 'Both sides have adopted rigid positions, with RPF presenting preconditions that RGF [Government of Rwanda] rejects … I regretfully have concluded that there is no prospect of a cease-fire being agreed upon in the coming days' (ibid). It must be noted that the UNSC was concerned with the question of how UNAMIR could assist in obtaining a cease-fire, but rarely touched upon the fate of the Rwandans or how UNAMIR could respond to the crimes against humanity being perpetrated, except for those small 'humanitarian pockets' that were under its control and where Tutsi civilians had sought refuge (Des Forges 1999: 625–8).

The UN Secretary-General presented the options to the UNSC members to permit them to reach a decision on 'whether, and if so how, the United Nations will maintain its efforts to help a people who have fallen into calamitous circumstances' (UN Doc S/1994/470). The Secretary-General offered three alternatives for the consideration of the UNSC.

> The first alternative is predicated on the conclusion … that there is no realistic prospect of the two opposing forces agreeing on an effective cease-fire in the immediate future. Without a cease-fire, combat between them will continue and so will the lawlessness and the massacres of civilians. This situation could only be changed by the immediate and massive reinforcement of UNAMIR and a change in its mandate so that it would be equipped and authorised to coerce the opposing forces into a cease-fire, and to attempt to restore law and order and put an end to the killings. This also would make possible the provision and distribution of humanitarian assistance by humanitarian agencies and non-governmental organisations not only in the capital, but in other parts of the country where the population has been displaced or subjected to deprivation as a result of the violence. Further, the restoration of stability in Rwanda would assist in preventing the repercussions of the violence from spreading to neighbouring countries and leading to regional instability. This scenario would require several thousand additional troops and UNAMIR may have to be given enforcement powers under Chapter VII of the Charter of the United Nations … I should report that the Permanent Representative of Rwanda to the United Nations called on

> me on 19 April with a plea to reinforce UNAMIR to enable it to end the chaos in his country.
>
> (ibid)

The Secretary-General thereafter continued with his second alternative to the UNSC:

> … a small group headed by the Force Commander, with necessary staff, would remain in Kigali to act as intermediary between the two parties in an attempt to bring them to an agreement on a cease-fire, this effort being maintained for a period of up to two weeks or longer, should the Council so prefer. Additional tasks would include assistance in the resumption of humanitarian relief operations to the extent feasible in this situation. UNAMIR has received assurances from both sides that they will cooperate in such operations, though there can be no certainty that this will be done. The team would require the support of an infantry company to provide security, as well as a number of military observers to monitor the situation, apart from civilian staff, the total being estimated at about 270. The remainder of UNAMIR personnel would be withdrawn, but UNAMIR, as a mission, would continue to exist.
>
> (ibid)

The Secretary-General in his report thereafter outlined the third alternative, namely the complete withdrawal of UNAMIR from Rwanda, which he made clear he did 'not favour':

> In view of the extreme nature and dimensions of the violence and mass killings over the last two weeks, there is little ground for hope that effective commitments could be obtained [that both sides would take measures to ensure the safety of civilians in the areas under their respective control] and it must be kept in mind that the consequences of complete withdrawal, in terms of human lives lost, could be very severe indeed. There could also be similar repercussions in neighbouring countries where citizens of the ethnic groups found in Rwanda reside.
>
> (ibid)

The Secretary-General's preference was for the first option, i.e. strengthening UNAMIR, this preference being expressed orally to the UNSC by the Secretary-General's Political Adviser, Chinmaya Gharekhan (UN Doc S/1999/1257). Nigeria presented a draft resolution on behalf of the non-aligned caucus, the group of non-aligned UN Member States. The resolution advocated the strengthening of UNAMIR, but it was never tabled in the UNSC because the United Kingdom and the United States, with power of veto, strongly opposed this option. Instead, British UN Ambassador Hannay intimated there were four possible options to deal with the situation in Rwanda. The first option was to increase the number of peacekeepers and to strengthen the mandate of UNAMIR to include peace enforcement; however, Hannay advised the UNSC that this option would potentially lead to a debacle akin to that in Somalia around six months previously. His second option was to provide UNAMIR with a mandate permitting it to stay on without any change to its composition and mandate, but Hannay questioned whether there was any value or purpose in retaining UNAMIR, arguing that with this mandate it would have no capability to save civilians. Hannay's two remaining options were pulling out UNAMIR completely, or retaining a skeletal force in Rwanda. Hannay had very much taken the lead on this situation within the UNSC, and indeed it was he who dictated that, taking all into account, the fourth option would be the best. The United States agreed wholeheartedly with the British stance (Interviews with former ambassadors to UNSC, 2006).

The permanent members of the UNSC with power of veto, namely the United States, the United Kingdom and Russia, preferred the option of partial withdrawal of UNAMIR; the majority of non-permanent members in the UNSC preferred the option of bolstering both the numbers of peacekeepers in Rwanda and the mandate provided to UNAMIR.

Discussions within the UNSC were heated. When interviewed, Hannay stated that:

> This was the point when the Americans [US delegation to UNSC] received these completely barmy instructions which was that the whole force [UNAMIR] had to be pulled out … When Madeleine [Albright, the US Ambassador to the United Nations] told me that, she said to me, 'Look I have got these instructions', and I said, 'Madeleine you can't do it you know, you just can't do it. There is a force there, the Ghanaians, there is a General [Dallaire] who is prepared to stay. We must stabilise the situation at the very least, but if we withdraw when we know that terrible things are happening, well … ' and she [Albright] got her instructions changed. All that has been documented a good deal as you know, but the brunt of the blame has been given to the Americans, rather unfairly in my view. And the outcome of that was the infamous Resolution [912], which everyone always describes as the Security Council's withdrawal of UNAMIR. The Security Council didn't withdraw UNAMIR, UNAMIR collapsed. The Security Council passed a resolution basically saying the force that is in Kigali is to stay there, but it was a tiny force, of course, 500 or something, mainly Ghanaians with some Tunisians and some others … It was a stabilisation measure; it was not an instruction to withdraw. The Security Council never decided to withdraw; the two battalions withdrew themselves as they had the right to do. Troop contributors always have that right. The Security Council

> merely decided that UNAMIR would stay but that it would basically stay in that run-down condition until we could get more people. So that is very often misrepresented.
>
> (Interview with Hannay, London, 2006)

And so it was that, on 21 April 1994, the UNSC unanimously adopted Resolution 912, in which it stated that it was ' ... appalled at the ensuing large-scale violence in Rwanda, which has resulted in the death of thousands of innocent civilians, including women and children' (UN Doc S/RES/912). The UNSC advised that owing to its 'deep concern for the safety and security of UNAMIR' it had reached an agreement to adjust the UNAMIR mandate to the following in keeping with the second alternative suggested by the Secretary-General in his letter of 20 April 1994:

> a) To act as an intermediary between the parties in an attempt to secure their agreement to a cease-fire; b) To assist in the resumption of humanitarian relief operations to the extent feasible; and c) To monitor and report on developments in Rwanda, including the safety and security of the civilians who sought refuge with UNAMIR, and authorises a force level as set out in paragraphs 15 to 18 of the Secretary-General's report of 20 April 1994 for that purpose.
>
> (ibid)

Resolution 912 was agreed on 21 April 1994 and, consequently, UNAMIR troops were infamously reduced from 2,700 to 270. It must be acknowledged that the final decision taken by the UNSC was predicated on the civil war between the FAR and the RPF, not on the systematic genocide of Tutsi civilians by the interim government of Hutu extremists. Although the UNSC record is silent on China's views here, Beijing, in common with other members, displayed no appetite to characterise the unfolding events as a genocide, instead acquiescing to the Security Council's characterisation of the crisis as a civil war (Welsh 2008).

It is irrefutable that Lord Hannay, played a significant role within the UNSC when the UNAMIR mandate was reviewed on 21 April 1994, and hence ultimately in the decision reached to drastically reduce the strength of UNAMIR in Rwanda as per Resolution 912. It was Hannay who rationalized to the UNSC that it was inadvisable to strengthen the mandate to include peace enforcement in case it resulted in a repetition of the debacle in Somalia.[18] The so-called 'Mogadishu Factor' (Robertson 2002). Hannay also argued against leaving the UNAMIR mandate unchanged, disputing that it was capable of saving lives. This left the two remaining options of either removing UNAMIR completely or retaining UNAMIR in Rwanda as 'a small skeletal force'. As previously noted, the United Kingdom supported the option to downsize UNAMIR to a skeletal force of 270 personnel and not to altering the mandate to permit peace enforcement.

One former UNSC delegate (Interview, 2006) was of the opinion that during the discussion on the future of UNAMIR on 21 April, the Council formed 'two camps', namely those favouring intervention, led by Nigeria, New Zealand and the Czech Republic; and those insisting on a complete withdrawal, led by the United States and the United Kingdom. When asked about the assertions of there being two factions within the UNSC, Colin Keating, the President of the Security Council, April 1994 responded:

> I would say that [this] is actually a snapshot of a particular day or couple of days and if you looked at it across weeks or months there is kind of a – and here I am talking about it from my perception of the British position – it wasn't a straight line, it sort of oscillated, and it partly oscillated in response to changing situations and levels of information … I think though that it is fair to say that the British position did sort of evolve … to being a more neutral position as the time went on.
>
> (Interview, New York, 2006)

Lord Hannay strongly disputes that two camps had formed within the UNSC:

> That's a lie! That is a simple lie. We did not favour withdrawal. And as I mentioned, I was the one that probably got Madeleine [Albright] to change her instructions round. They [the US] only very briefly favoured withdrawal but they did make a lot of policy mistakes, the Americans. First of all, they sent her instructions saying they favoured withdrawal. That lasted 24 hours and then she turned the instructions around and they [US representatives] then voted for the maintenance of UNAMIR. Then when the discussions were going on about what should be done they had this completely barmy idea that any new force should operate from outside Rwanda, and should not go into Rwanda and should merely concentrate in ensuring that the refugee camps and so on were safe. Well, that was totally barmy considering that people were being murdered by the thousands inside Rwanda and you couldn't establish a ring of ringside seats around Rwanda to watch this happening, and so one was gradually worn down, and then they basically came on board for UNAMIR II. But that is incorrect, that description about the two camps.
>
> (Interview, London, 2006)

Keating states 'it was inevitable that Resolution 912 of April 21, 1994, which decided to downsize the UNAMR force, would be misunderstood and criticized. But even with the benefit of hindsight, I still consider it the only viable option at that time with any possibility of a good outcome' (Malone 2004: 508).

Discussion within the House of Commons clearly highlights that the British Ambassador's role within the UNSC was inkeeping with British policy and his stance was in accordance with the will of the Cabinet and the

Foreign Secretary. Indeed, when asked in Parliament to explain British Government approval of the reduction in strength of UNAMIR, and if there is 'one level of compassion for our European friends in Bosnia and another for Black Africans' (Hansard Parliamentary Debates, 25 April 1994). Foreign Secretary Hurd replied:

> I am not sure how ... maintaining a United Nations force on the original scale will help assuage those horrors. Have not they read the report by the Secretary-General on which the Security Council acted? The Security Council concluded, on the advice of the Secretary-General, that it was no longer possible for the United Nations force to carry out its mandate in the form expected ... there is no magic in keeping troops there if there is nothing useful that they can do ... The effort must be to bring an end to the fighting. That cannot be achieved, as has been proved, by the United Nations force on the ground.
>
> (ibid)

Hannay contradicts that account:

> I think, you know, that if we had had any idea of what was happening [in Rwanda] we ought to have produced some troops to strengthen UNAMIR. I mean it couldn't be said that we didn't have them; of course we had some troops even although we were heavily engaged in Bosnia. We should all have done so, the Americans should have done, we should have done, and other Europeans should have done and so on ... we should have backed intervention. I mean, if we believe now in the 'responsibility to protect', well you can't read that back to then, but in retrospect, of course, there was a responsibility by the international community to protect the Tutsis because they were not being protected by their own government.
>
> (Interview, London, 2006)

In the meantime, meetings between the RPF and President Museveni were continuing in an effort to supposedly put pressure on the RPF to agree to a cease-fire. A further meeting had been arranged between the General Secretary of the RPF, Museveni, and the Rwandan and US Ambassadors to Uganda. 'Museveni readily agreed to invite me [Clay] to join the group, and we also agreed it might be prudent to invite the French ambassador' (Cable, Kampala to London, 20 April 1994).

The result of this meeting was a draft initiative for a cease-fire proposed by Museveni with the approval of the British High Commissioner, albeit not all Museveni's suggestions were accepted. This information was relayed from Kampala by cable to London and the UKMIS NY on 24 April 1994. Both parties, namely the RPF and GOR representative, 'were tasked to put the proposal to their respective authorities and to report back with their reactions to President Museveni on Saturday morning. ... we should keep alongside Museveni and encourage him to remain engaged with RPF' (ibid). A communication forwarded from Kampala to London confirmed the text of the final draft of the proposal for Museveni to put to the RPF and the GOR. Clay noted that the RPF representative had proven quite difficult whilst the GOR had been accepting of the proposals. Clay stated 'I reminded the meeting that Rudasingwa's [RPF General Secretary] attempts to introduce discussion of quote legitimacy unquote and to qualify the word quote violence unquote would be seen by world opinion as distractions from the overwhelming need to stop the killings' (Cable, Kampala to London, 21 April 1994). London was advised by their High Commissioner in Kampala that, 'He [Museveni] told Rudasingwa the prospects of getting a decent settlement in Rwanda were better from the RPF's point of view that they had ever been. The RPF should not risk their advantage by flouting world opinion'. Edward Clay was then invited by Museveni to attend the meeting of 24 April 1994 (ibid).

Non-governmental organisation press releases indicated the extent of the atrocity and ongoing massacres in Rwanda. On 21 April, an ICRC press release indicated 'the fighting that has raged in central Rwanda since early April has now spread to the entire country ... Tens maybe hundreds of thousands killed: the exact number of victims of the massacres that have swept Rwanda over the last two weeks will never be known ... The human tragedy in Rwanda is on a scale that the International Red Cross has rarely witnessed'.[19] The following day, Oxfam issued a statement condemning the UNSC decision to drastically reduce UNAMIR numbers in Rwanda. Some two weeks after the start of the violence, Oxfam estimated in its press release that over 100,000 people had been killed.[20] On 26 April, Amnesty International released a press statement saying that 'government and security force officials are ordering the killing in Rwanda and the international community should act to stop them'.[21] An ICRC press release of 28 April called on all governments concerned, including all members of the UNSC, to take all possible measures to end the massacres; on the same day, Oxfam issued a press release stating that 'Oxfam fear genocide is happening in Rwanda', based on the content of phone communications from staff in Burundi's border with Rwanda.[22] These press releases proved to be somewhat inflammatory and, on 29 April 1994, an extended UNSC debate took place to discuss the use of the word 'genocide' in an outgoing UNSC Presidential Statement. The United Kingdom and United States resisted the use of the word genocide (Interviews with members of 1994 UNSC), but the UNSC nevertheless acknowledged that 'massacres and wanton killings ... in a systematic manner' were occurring (UN Doc S/PV.337). On 29 April, the ICRC issued the most strongly worded statement in its history demanding that the UNSC take action, and wrote to the FCO to draw its attention to the tragic situation in

Rwanda, stating that its statement was 'an initiative addressed simultaneously to several Governments in a position to influence the course of events in Rwanda, urging them to act without delay to bring an end to the massacres'.[23]

In a letter, also dated 29 April 1994, the UN Secretary-General informed the UNSC 'that the Force Commander of the United Nations Assistance Mission for Rwanda has reported a further deterioration of the situation in Kigali and other parts of Rwanda ... UNAMIR reports strong evidence of preparations for further massacres of civilians in the city and there are several large concentrations of civilians who fear for their lives but enjoy little effective protection' (UN Doc S/1995/518).

As such, the Secretary-General questioned the revised mandate to reduce the number of troops stationed in Rwanda with UNAMIR, which was agreed in Resolution 912 on 21 April 1994 drastically reducing the number of troops stationed in Rwanda with UNAMIR. The Secretary-General wrote:

> It has become clear that that mandate does not give UNAMIR the power to take effective action to halt the continuing massacres. ... according to some estimates, as many as 200,000 people may have died during the last three weeks. This humanitarian catastrophe is rightly a matter of growing anguish in Africa and the rest of the world and demands urgent action by the international community. ... The events of the last few days have confirmed however that UNAMIR's revised mandate is not one which enables it to bring massacres under control. ... It has become clear that the horrors ... can be ended only if law and order is restored, a task which is far beyond UNAMIR's present capacity. In these circumstances I urge the Security Council to re-examine the decisions which it took in Resolution 912 and to consider again what action, including forceful action, it could take, or could authorise Member States to take, in order to restore law and order and end the massacres. In making this recommendation, I am of course aware that such action would require a commitment of human and material resources on a scale, which Member States have so far proved reluctant to contemplate. But I am convinced that the scale of human suffering in Rwanda and its implications for the stability of neighbouring countries leaves the Security Council with no alternative but to examine this possibility.
>
> (ibid)

General political will

For several weeks after the agreement of Resolution 912, there was continuing pressure on the permanent members of the UNSC to initiate an intervention in Rwanda. Albeit subject to debate, several independent reports and individual actors have stated that the genocide could have been prevented or stopped had the international community possessed sufficient collective will (Burkhalter 1994; Annan 2000; UN Doc S/1999/1257).

Senior members of the Major Government of 1994 were questioned about the lack of such an initiation to intervene by the UNSC. In response, one senior politician stated, 'If there is a *general* political will by the international community, *almost any* dispute can be stopped … however, as a former colonial power Britain has generally been reluctant to intervene unilaterally' [my emphasis] (Interview, London, 2006).

This was disputed by Lillian Wong, a senior member of the FCO staff in 1994, who argued that 'it was not a general lack of political will that prevented intervention', reasoning instead that it was 'a combination of legal obligations, national interests, humanitarian considerations, public pressure, practicality – and you've got to work out a combination of these' (Interview, London, 2006).

Another member of Major's Cabinet also asserted that, in the case of Rwanda, the lack of intervention from the international community was not solely because of a lack of political will. Contrary to the response of the previous interviewee, however, he reasoned that a British intervention to stop genocide in Rwanda did not occur 'merely because the facts had not been established' (Interview, London, 2006), and continued:

> There are always two sides to the argument … I don't think the problem was simply lack of political will … I'm not trying to say that there was criticism not to be made of the international community. I think the international community didn't find out, it didn't make enough effort to find out what was going on and perhaps didn't want to. Not because it was afraid of what it might discover but simply because it was preoccupied elsewhere. … [L]ike everybody else, we saw the press reports and we were aware of the fact that there was clearly loss of life taking place. I don't think any of us were aware of the … I have to choose my words carefully, I don't think … any of us would have been absolutely certain as to the scale of what was happening … I don't think I appreciated or accepted that that meant there was a sustained and deliberate desire to massacre every possible person they could find in that. … it sounds so terrible, sounds so awful, you tend to assume it can't be quite that bad and the information coming out of Rwanda was mixed, I mean, it was all anecdotal because of the very nature of what was happening there. The contacts were limited so you had journalists, some of whom were getting very graphic reports of a very dramatic event, so I think I would sum that up by saying we knew there were horrible things happening. I think that it would be correct to say that we didn't

> appreciate the full scale until later of what was happening and the sheer intensity of it.
>
> (ibid)

As previously noted, the RPF had made clear that it was able to deal with the situation in Rwanda without international intervention, and indeed it did not welcome UNAMIR intervention. The RPF had made significant advances quite rapidly and less than three weeks after the assassination of Habyarimana, the British High Commissioner in Kampala, cabled London and the UKMIS NY to advise that 'a visiting Belgian diplomat has meanwhile reported that three quarters of Kigali now appears to be under the control of the RPF … UNAMIR's strength has now been reduced to 430'[24] (Cable, Kampala to London, 26 April 1994). It was to be a further two months before the massacres would end (see Wertheim 2010 and 2011, for an insightful discussion regarding humanitarian intervention and Rwanda).

In Uganda, ceasefire discussions continued with President Museveni mediating between the RPF and representatives of the GOR. The British High Commissioner continued to be deeply involved in the ailing cease-fire negotiations. Museveni had been a central mediating figure throughout the fragile process of negotiating a cease-fire. However, President Mobutu of Zaire had also made various offers of assistance, which had been rejected. A cable from Kampala to London on 29 April 1994 states that 'regional initiatives (peace) are currently in disarray. Mobutu is running his own show as quote facilitator unquote, but it is essentially a spoiling game: he has so far given the RGF an alibi for failing to turn up at Arusha and the RPF for failing to negotiate at Arusha. Mobutu is perceived … as having the capacity to do harm but little to do good'. The following day, at the 3,371st meeting of the UNSC, the outgoing President stated on behalf of the Council, and as agreed by the Council, that it 'is appalled at continuing reports of the slaughter of innocent civilians in Kigali and other parts of Rwanda, and reported preparations for further massacres. It endorses the concern expressed by the Central Organ for Conflict Prevention, Management and Resolution of the OAU that the massacres and wanton killings have continued unabated in a systematic manner in Rwanda'. The statement quoted directly one sentence from the UNGC, but did not mention the word genocide.

On the same day, Claude Dusaidi, the RPF representative at the United Nations, issued a press release alleging that during February and March 1994, he provided 'detailed information … about militia training, arms dumps, political murders, hate propaganda, and death lists [to] … British diplomats' and other members of the UNSC.[25] When interviewed by the author, former permanent and non-permanent members of the UNSC recalled meeting with Claude Dusaidi (now deceased) in the corridors of the New York UN building in the weeks prior to the genocide. However, none would confirm or deny his claims about the information he purported to have shared.

On 3 May 1994, the Director of Oxfam, David Bryer, personally presented a letter to Prime Minister John Major at Downing Street, requesting intervention in Rwanda, and informing him that there was:

> genocide on an horrific scale with a level of killing the world has not seen since Cambodia in the 1970s ... For the most part, the death squads are armed with clubs and machetes, not guns, so I believe that even a relatively small UN force could offer protection to civilians seeking refuge in safe areas. ... This week, I was sent the enclosed fax from people hiding in the Hotel des Mille Collines in Kigali. The Hotel contains 500 people and is being protected by just 6 soldiers.[26]

Amnesty International issued a press release on 4 May indicating its overwhelming concern at the ongoing massacres in Rwanda. It had also written a letter to the British Ambassador to the UNSC, David Hannay, and asked him to respond on behalf of the United Kingdom to its press release. Hannay immediately forwarded a telex to London seeking instructions from the British Foreign Secretary, Douglas Hurd (Cable, UKMIS NY to London, 4 May 1994). The instructions issued by the FCO in response to this request remain classified, despite repeated FOI requests.

On 16 May 1994 the UNSC convened once again to discuss the Rwandan situation. Interviews with members of the UNSC of 1994 indicate that the British Ambassador, David Hannay, proved himself to be obstructive during this meeting when increasing the strength of UNAMIR was proposed (Interviews, 2006). Drawing analogies with Somalia, Hannay argued that to reinforce the peacekeepers in Rwanda, and provide a stronger mandate affording security and protection to the people of Rwanda, would court disaster. In accordance with the military tactics and demands of the RPF during meetings with British SIS in Uganda, Hannay made clear to the UNSC that this was an African problem that required an African solution (ibid). Despite Hannay's objections, Resolution 918 was approved by the UNSC the following day, authorising the expansion of the UN mission in Rwanda – now referred to as UNAMIR II – to 5,500 troops, with a mandate that permitted their contribution to security and protection.

It should, however, be noted that although the resolution authorised increasing force levels, it did not actually authorise deployment of 5,500 troops. In the text of Resolution 918, the UNSC intimated the:

> urgent need for coordinated action to alleviate suffering of the Rwanda people and help restore peace in Rwanda, and in this connection *welcoming* cooperation between the United Nations and the OAU as well as with

> countries of the region. ... [The UNSC] invites Member States to respond promptly to the Secretary-General's request for the resources required, including logistical support capability for rapid deployment of the UNAMIR expanded force level and its support in the field.
>
> (UN Doc S/Res/918)

The emphasis on 'welcoming' was in the original text, a document whose compilation was dominated by the US and the UK Ambassadors to the UNSC. Although Resolution 918 authorised expansion, there was to be phased implementation of the new mandate.

Phase I was to take place with immediate effect, with implementation of further phases were dependent on satisfactory update reports. The text of the document clearly 'invites Member States to respond promptly to the Secretary-General's request for the resources required, including logistical support capability for rapid deployment of the UNAMIR expanded force level and its support in the field'. It is apparent that the invitation was directed to all members and not just certain factions of the United Nations.

Such an increase in strength clearly required troops from UN Member States, and indeed there were sufficient offers from African countries, including Ghana, Ethiopia, Malawi, Senegal, Nigeria, Zimbabwe and Zambia. However, those countries required material equipment, APCs and airlifting. Supplies for the African troops were requested from Western governments, but they proved reluctant to fulfil this requirement.

As a permanent member of the UNSC, the United Kingdom was specifically asked to provide immediate logistical support for the Ghanaian and other African troops proffered to UNAMIR II, to enable the personnel to be deployed soonest and in any case within seven days of 17 May 1994. By 31 May, some two weeks after the authorisation of Phase I of Resolution 918 that should have witnessed the strengthening of UNAMIR II to 800 troops, no troops had yet arrived in Rwanda. This was due to the British Government and other members of the UNSC repeatedly refusing to acknowledge these urgent requests from the Secretariat for the provision of troops and/or logistical support to permit the speedy formation of UNAMIR II.

On the same day as the approval of Resolution 918, Oxfam issued a press release intimating its concern that Resolution 918 stipulated no deadline for the arrival of troops in Rwanda.[27] This was followed six days later with an Oxfam International press release announcing that it had sent a letter to President Clinton of the United States asking him 'not to delay urgent action to save lives in Rwanda' and describing itself as 'exasperated'.[28]

At a Press Conference in New York, 25 May 1994, the Secretary General intimated that over 200,000 people had been killed and expressed his frustration with the international community's refusal to act quickly, in particular by sending troops (UN Doc SG/SM/5292).

Oxfam issued a further press release on 26 May 1994, in which it 'condemns months of inactivity by Governments as genocide rages in Rwanda'.[29] So far, three African Governments, namely Ghana, Senegal and Ethiopia, had made firm commitments to supply a total of 2,200 troops to the UN force in Rwanda, but no government, including those contributing troops, seemed willing to provide the planes to immediately get them there or the equipment they might need. One Oxfam spokesperson stated in the press release that 'it is bad enough that hardly any governments have offered troops. It is even worse that no one seems willing to pay for those troops that have been offered … we are entitled to ask what has been done by governments in the past month, and especially in the last fortnight since Resolution 918 of the UN Security Council authorised 5,500 extra troops'.[30]

The Secretary-General declared on 31 May that what had occurred in Rwanda constituted genocide (UN Doc S/1994/640). However, Phase 1 of Resolution 918 had still not taken effect and no troops had arrived in Rwanda. The Secretary-General advised all Member States that Ghana was prepared to dispatch the required troops immediately, but pointed out that this deployment would be pointless without proper equipment, particularly armoured personnel carriers. He thereafter requested that the UNSC consider initiating phase II of Resolution 918 in close synchronisation with Phase I because of its projected long delay in deploying troop and equipment.

During an interview with a senior member of the FCO, it became evident to the author that throughout May 1994, almost all the information and intelligence in relation to the atrocities in Rwanda that was received at the FCO office was from Washington. Such an admission is of significance in respect of the 'special relationship' that is both historical and current between the United States and United Kingdom, and the role of that relationship in the Rwandan genocide. The exact pathway for detailed reports of the situation on the ground in Rwanda and other intelligence was as follows: Washington – UKMIS NY – London – Kampala. Unfortunately, the FCO has taken the decision not to declassify this intelligence. This undoubtedly leaves substantial gaps in our understanding of the content and relevancy of the intelligence that the British Government would have been in possession of throughout May 1994, the instructions issued to British diplomatic staff in Kampala and surrounding states, and also to intelligence operatives.

It was on 17 June that France announced its plan to the UNSC to deploy a mission to Rwanda as an interim peacekeeping force, hoping that its proposed resolution would receive agreement from the Security Council. Two days later, on 19 June 1994, the Secretary-General issued a letter to the President of the UNSC articulating his growing frustration that Phases I and II of Resolution 918 had still to be implemented. He stated:

> The Secretariat has still not been able to secure offers for medical and other support units. In the absence of firm commitments for military

> logistical units, it will be necessary to seek a civilian contractor on an emergency basis … until the necessary logistic support from Governments can be secured … It should be noted that none of those Governments possessing the capacity to provide fully trained and equipped military units have offered so far to do so for the implementation of the Security Council's resolutions to deal with the situation in Rwanda. In the light of the above, it is evident that, with the failure of Member States to promptly provide the resources necessary for the implementation of its expanded mandate, UNAMIR may not be in a position for about three months to fully undertake the tasks entrusted to it by those resolutions. Meanwhile the situation in Rwanda has continued to deteriorate and the killing of innocent civilians has not stopped.
>
> (UN Doc S/1994/728)

It was in this climate of inactivity by international nations that a report was released on 28 June 1994 by the Special Rapporteur, appointed some four weeks previously to report on the human rights situation in Rwanda. His detailed assessment confirmed that genocide and other human rights violations had indeed occurred in the country (UN Doc E/CN.4/1995/7).

Chapter 7

How Britain Responded

> Great power and great crimes are inseparable. It is only those with great political or economic power who can, with the stroke of a pen, an utterance of an order, or even a knowing nod of the head, send thousands to their death or consign millions to lives of unrelenting want and misery. When economic and political powers pursue common interests, the potential for harm is magnified further.
>
> (Michalowski and Kramer 2006: 1)

As the previous chapter has demonstrated, a British and US intelligence network was developed and sustained in the Great Lakes region of Africa throughout the 1990s; the United Kingdom's diplomatic relationship with Uganda and France necessitated that it keep abreast of events in Central Africa. The research has presented evidence that the British Government was privy to a wealth of relevant and reliable intelligence, both before and during the genocide, knowledge that would have given the United Kingdom a clear perspective on the extent of the violence in Rwanda throughout the 1990s, and the role of the RPF and the Government of Uganda in the conflict.

The positive decision of the British Government not to act to prevent or stop the outbreak of uncontrolled violence and genocide in Rwanda when faced with substantial reliable information has been explained and excused in varying manners by diplomatic staff and members of the Cabinet. In his published memoirs, Sir Douglas Hurd, Foreign Secretary states in reference to the tragedy in Rwanda, 'We acted throughout in good conscience, though that in itself is not itself a justification for particular decisions. We made mistakes' (2004: 493).

British policy: double standards exist

Within five days of the assassination of Rwanda's President and the start of the genocide, Hurd explained in Parliament that it was 'proximity' that dictated the British Government's expenditure of energy and resources in response to the civil war in Bosnia and its lack of response to Rwanda's ongoing plight. He continued, 'The civil war in Bosnia and the suffering in the former Yugoslavia are in our continent. They are quite close to us. It is right we should be devoting such effort to them' (Hansard Parliamentary Debates, 12 April 1994). When interviewed by the author, several members of the 1994 Cabinet believed still that their lack of response to the atrocities in Rwanda in 1994 was justifiable, withone senior member of the 1994 Cabinet stating:

> Douglas was simply being starkly honest about our incapacity to act on too wide a front. We had to judge where we could be most efficient ... the three-sided civil war in former Yugoslavia was a different case [to Rwanda]. We were aware of the dangers of the civil war as well as the inhumanities being perpetrated on the borders of the European Union. The judgment we made was that in these circumstances we could make a difference.
>
> (Interview, London, 2007)

Another added that inaction was justifiable in Rwanda since it was 'on a different continent' (Interview, London, 2006).

One senior British Government minister explained, 'I was struggling with the Bosnia problem which raised many of the same issues [as Rwanda] but was very much on our own doorstep ... we [the British Government] are instinctively very cautious; reluctant to believe that putting in white European troops from former colonial powers into a war situation in an African country is likely to be helpful' (Interview, London, 2006).

Such opinions were not shared across Government. One senior staff member of the FCO described Hurd's comments to Parliament as 'appalling', and continued, 'it's a pretty strange statement to have made because Britain is one of the five permanent members of the Security Council, so we do have an obligation to police the world, so to speak, and be informed about it. So, that is a pretty uninformed statement, let's put it that way ... it implies that Africa doesn't matter' (Interview, London, 2006).

Another member of John Major's Cabinet who also argued against such a governmental policy towards Rwanda stated:

> My disagreement was why are we prepared to do so much in one area [Bosnia] and not in another [Rwanda]. And it is proximity, yes, you're right. You know, small country, middle of a great big continent, it's not terribly friendly, don't have the resources, have to make hard decisions; so, in a sense, ethics almost didn't come into it ... At a meeting I told them [Cabinet] they [the Rwandans] are mad with killing fever and you have to intervene. You cannot stop this unless you physically intervene and I can remember being challenged about putting British soldiers to their death in a foreign land. I had a battle royal. It all came down to

> resources and British interest and demands on British troops. It's all the same story.
>
> (Interview, London, 2006)

When questioned on proximity-dependent policies, one former British Ambassador to the UKMIS NY stated, 'It's difficult to do this in a public domain because it sounds so terrible … Double standards exist, but that doesn't mean to say you don't help where you can' (Interview, London, 2006).

'We will not call this genocide'

For the first four weeks of massacres in Rwanda, the UNSC did not discuss genocide, despite strong evidence indicating a systematic campaign of extermination of Tutsis. Had the crisis been labelled by the UNSC as 'genocide,' then all the members of the Council would have been bound to act under the terms of the UNGC.

At an informal meeting of the UNSC on 29 April 1994 to discuss the potential of setting up a war crimes tribunal in relation to the atrocities committed in Rwanda, much of the debate concerned the Council's recognition and use of the word 'genocide' (Interview with UNSC member, London, 2006). The outgoing President, Colin Keating, had tabled a draft Presidential Statement in the UNSC that referred to the Rwandan conflict as genocide. It was supported by four of the other non-permanent members, namely New Zealand, the Czech Republic, Argentina and Spain (ibid).

A Presidential Statement requires the consensus of all members of the UNSC, and as such Keating's proposal was dismissed due to vehement opposition from the British, American and Chinese representatives, who strenuously objected to the use of the word 'genocide' to describe the ongoing situation in Rwanda; 'there was a lot of what might be called theoretical opposition to the use of the term [genocide] based on reluctance to categorise in a legal sense what was' (ibid). The British Ambassador's stance at the meeting was in keeping with British policy and in accordance with the official instructions of the Foreign Secretary.

Their objections were accepted within the UNSC, albeit reluctantly by many of the Member States, and a declaration was adopted in the early hours of 30 April, which condemned:

> all these breaches of international humanitarian law in Rwanda, particularly those perpetrated against the civilian population, and recalls that persons who instigate or participate in such acts are individually responsible. In this context, the Security Council recalls that the killing of members of an ethnic group with the intention of destroying such a group in whole or in part constitutes a crime punishable under international law.
>
> (UN Doc S/PRST/1994/21)

Despite using legal terminology from the UNGC, it rejected the use of the term 'genocide.' Interviews with former FCO staff and members of the British Cabinet of 1994 have revealed:

> It was Douglas Hurd who said 'We are not to call this genocide'. The reason is because that then brings up obligations under, you know, the Genocide Convention. Again, his mind was really somewhere else, but he would not allow it, and the American ... Madeleine Albright, she was totally against calling it genocide. I think we were very much following the American lead on this and, again, it was the New York discussions that kind of dominated the thinking here. I don't think the people at the desk level or even up to the head of department would have necessarily advised on such a floppy policy but it was definitely coming from the top, from Douglas Hurd.
>
> (Interviews, London, 2006)

One former Cabinet member recalls that, during a Cabinet meeting in July 1994, Foreign Secretary Hurd 'thump[ed] the table once and said "We will not call this genocide"'. The refusal of the United Kingdom to recognise what is now defined as genocide was:

> Because the lawyers claimed that in international law, that as soon as you use the word genocide, then you are bound to take certain actions and they [the United Kingdom] didn't have the resource to take those action ... that is basically the reason, because of the international law and the obligations and such like so it wasn't the fact that they just didn't think that it was genocide.
>
> (Interview, London, 2006)

One FCO diplomat who was something of an expert on African issues, and particularly those relating to Rwanda, indicated that:

> we [the FCO] kept referring the issue [use of the word genocide to describe events in Rwanda] to some committee of experts until they decided what actually happened and dictated we weren't going to use this word [genocide]. It was Douglas Hurd who was responsible for this, by the way – it's not people at the bottom, it definitely came from the top.
>
> (Interview, London, 2006)

One year after the atrocities in Rwanda, the FCO sent a letter to an international inquiry saying that it still did not accept the term genocide. It said that it saw a discussion about whether the massacres constituted genocide as 'sterile' (Curtis 2003: 360).

Misrepresentations

Evidence indicates that the Conservative Government also made misrepresentations in Parliament. The Douglas Hurd was asked by Tony Worthington MP in the House of Commons 'what recent requests the Secretary-General of the United Nations has made to the Security Council members about upgrading the UN involvement in Rwanda; and what was his response' (Hansard Parliamentary Debates, 9 May 1994). The Under Secretary of State for Foreign and Commonwealth Affairs, Mark Lennox-Boyd, responded 'the UN Secretary-General has made no requests to the Security Council about upgrading United Nations involvement in Rwanda' (ibid).

This was wholly inaccurate: in a letter dated 29 April 1994, the UN Secretary-General addressed Member States, to inform them of the further deterioration of conditions in Rwanda and strong evidence of preparations for further massacres of civilians. The Secretary-General questioned the revised mandate agreed in Resolution 912 on 21 April 1994, which drastically reduced the number of troops stationed in Rwanda with UNAMIR (UN Doc S/518/1994). The Secretary-General wrote:

> … it has become clear that that mandate does not give UNAMIR the power to take effective action to halt the continuing massacres … This humanitarian catastrophe is rightly a matter of growing anguish in Africa and the rest of the world and demands urgent action by the international community … The events of the last few days have confirmed however that UNAMIR's revised mandate is not one which enables it to bring massacres under control … It has become clear that the horrors … can be ended only if law and order is restored, a task which is far beyond UNAMIR's present capacity. In these circumstances I urge the Security Council to re-examine the decisions which it took in resolution 912 and to consider again what action, including forceful action, it could take, or could authorise Member States to take, in order to restore law and order and end the massacres. In making this recommendation, I am of course aware that such action would require a commitment of human and material resources on a scale, which Member States have so far proved reluctant to contemplate. But I am convinced that the scale of human suffering in Rwanda and its implications for the stability of neighbouring countries leaves the Security Council with no alternative but to examine this possibility.
>
> (ibid)

Despite the United Kingdom being a permanent member of the UNSC, the British Government misrepresented to Parliament requests made of it by the Secretary-General, and then failed to acknowledge urgent requests from the Secretariat for the provision of troops and/or logistical support to permit the speedy formation of UNAMIR II; and specifically, immediate logistical support for the proffered Ghanaian troops to allow them to be deployed soonest and in any case within seven days of 17 May 1994.

This is, however, disputed by some members of the 1994 Major Government, who are of the opinion that the logistics forwarded by the United Kingdom to Rwanda were 'very valuable once it was provided' (Interview, London, 2006). One former Cabinet member indicated that:

> the UK contribution to the international response was proportionate and was reasonable. Whether the international response itself was adequate is a different matter, and I go back to the point that, I'm repeating myself, that clearly I think the mistake that was made by the international community, including the United Kingdom, was not to find out early enough the scale of what was happening in order to judge whether some much more substantial response was needed.
>
> (Interview, London, 2006)

It has been further suggested that explaining the British Government's response to the knowledge and options available has to be viewed in the knowledge that British policy in relation to Rwanda was being made in response to guidelines and intelligence coming from New York, circumstances described by one FCO diplomat as 'interesting because that's a very unusual situation. But it was so' (Interview, London, 2006).

It was almost three months after the start of the genocide in Rwanda that John Major made his first statement regarding the atrocities during Prime Minister's Question Time in the House of Commons on 7 July 1994. When questioned about the lack of British military support towards the strengthening of UNAMIR II, Major explained 'It is simply not practicable for it [the UNSC] to become the policeman of every part of the world' (Hansard Parliamentary Debates, 7 July 1994). One week later, however, the Under Secretary for State for the FCO advised Parliament 'we are fully joining in international efforts to bring a halt to the bloodshed ... We have offered 50 trucks to the United Nations Aid Mission in Rwanda, UNAMIR' – much to the hilarity of the Conservative MPs (Hansard Parliamentary Debates, 13 July 1994).

On being questioned further in Parliament by Tony Worthington MP, about 'the wholly inadequate offer of supplementary logistical support', Lennox-Boyd responded 'I can only reiterate that the provision of British equipment is the result of what has been requested of us by the United Nations ... the troops sought by the Secretary-General are coming from a number of African countries, which I think is right ... it is not lack of support from the British Government that is constraining activities in that area [formation of UNAMIR II]' (ibid).

The Force Commander of UNAMIR is scathing of the British contribution, stating:

> The British offered 50 Bedford trucks ... for a sizeable amount [of monies] to be paid [to the British Government] upfront. The Bedford is an early Cold War-era truck, which in 1994 was fit only to be a museum relic ... The British later quietly withdrew their request for payment and provided some of the vehicles, which broke down one at a time until there were none left.
>
> (Dallaire 2004: 376)

The Secretary of Defence, Malcolm Rifkind, was asked in Parliament by Peter Luff MP, 'what requests he has received to provide troops for peace-keeping purposes in Rwanda' (Hansard Parliamentary Debates, 19 July 1994). He responded, '[w]e have received no requests to provide troops for the United Nations operation in Rwanda ... ' (ibid). Questioning in Parliament continued when Rifkind was asked to 'assure the House that any requests for specialist military assistance that may be forthcoming will be looked on as sympathetically as possible' (ibid). Despite Rifkind's explicit intention that there would be no British support for any peace operation in Rwanda, his public representation in Parliament was, 'Yes, naturally we would do so because we understand the scale of the human tragedy that is unfolding in Rwanda' (ibid). Rifkind continued 'I am sure the United Kingdom can hold its head high for the contribution that it is making in helping to minimise the dreadful suffering in Rwanda' (ibid). As a result of the lack of provision of equipment to permit the formation of UNAMIR II, its launch was delayed until the genocide was virtually over. But why did the British Government respond in such a manner and opt for the aforementioned responses? Would such actions be definable as complicity in the crimes committed against the people of Rwanda in 1994 by omission?

As noted earlier in this chapter, the United Kingdom had no economic interests in Rwanda prior to the genocide. However, there *was* political interest in the civil war of 1990 onwards as a result of the close relationship that the British Government had nurtured with Uganda, Rwanda's close neighbour, due in no small part to the economic interests that the British Government held in Uganda. British interest in the turbulence in Rwanda was also due to the RPF's close relationship with Uganda and allegations of support from Museveni. It should be noted that, although Museveni denied these allegations at the time, during the '15th Liberation Anniversary' on 4 July 2009, Museveni delivered a speech explaining his substantial role and that of the Ugandan NRA in the liberation of Rwanda in 1994, stating that 'he created the situation where by RPA was never defeated' (BBC Monitoring Africa 2009).

Was Britain compliant?

This chapter has revealed the 'close' relationship that had developed throughout the early 1990s between the RPF and the British High Commission in Kampala, a relationship that produced 'excellent and very strong intelligence', which was relayed to London as a matter of course. What is still not apparent is to what degree this relationship was mutually beneficial.

As previously outlined, throughout the 1990s, both before and after the arrival of Edward Clay as High Commissioner in Kampala, the RPF was warning the British diplomats there of 'impending tragedy … catastrophe' – detail that was communicated to London. What is of note, however, is that the RPF was perceived as being rather skilled in the art of manipulation and, as previously noted, its warnings were perceived by the High Commission in Uganda as exaggeration and 'crying wolf'. According to one British official from the office in Kampala, it was just not possible to make any 'real assessment' of the information being passed from the RPF. Its warnings could not be triangulated, albeit the intelligence forwarded from this group of rebels was without fail forwarded to London. One diplomat explained that 'failing to recognise the validity of those warnings was at least a failure of information and of understanding and analysis' (Interview, London, 2006). British Cabinet members stated, 'we knew very little about it. It wasn't a country which we had ever been closely involved and so there really was no knowledge' (Interview, London, 2006), and 'there was neither great knowledge nor great pressure' (Interview, London, 2006).

The general consensus of the elite interviewees who were members of the British Government during the period immediately prior to, and during the genocide in Rwanda, is that they themselves were largely uninformed, lacking in any semblance of reliable or relevant information about events in Rwanda.

This book has endeavoured to establish British foreign policy towards Rwanda in the period before and during the genocide of 1994, and the factors giving rise to such decision-making. It has provided detailed insight into not only the nature and extent of the warnings available to the British Government, but also the source, and as such the quality of the intelligence and information available to them, both before and during the genocide. Significant to the question under enquiry is the revelation that British foreign policy in the period prior to and during the actual atrocity appears to have been influenced by United States intelligence and its policy towards Rwanda. The United States and United Kingdom have historically shared intelligence information gathered both from overt and covert sources. The United Kingdom provides substantial quantities of intelligence to the United States; it is reported that the United Kingdom receives even greater amounts from the United States (Aldrich 1994).

The British Government was in receipt of ample information that would have permitted a clear insight into the deteriorating conditions in Rwanda. Reliable and relevant intelligence was being forwarded to the United Kingdom from Washington, though due to the ongoing censorship of much of the documentation it is not possible at this time to ascertain the exact content of much of that material.

In the 18 years since the genocide in Rwanda, the British Government has repeatedly excused its decisions and actions in respect of Rwanda by claiming to have had no prior interest in the country and no access to intelligence or information. Predicating its inaction on this basis is clearly inaccurate because UK diplomatic relationships with Uganda and France necessitated that the Government kept abreast of events in Central Africa. An intelligence network had been developed and sustained throughout the 1990s and the RPF was apparently provided with the opportunity to voice its opinion on UNAMIR's mandate prior to UNSC discussions.

Omission is only criminalised when there is a legal requirement imposing a clear obligation to act – as is found in Article I of the UNGC, which imposes an unconditional positive obligation on contracting parties to prevent genocide. It is apparent that the British Government *did* have knowledge and took a positive decision not to act to prevent genocide in Rwanda, and as such omitted to fulfil its obligations in terms of the UNGC and international law. The evidence presented here builds a case to show that the positive steps undertaken by the UK Government in negating its legal responsibilities can be summarised as follows:

- Arguing that Rwanda was on a different continent, which negated the very real and documented dangers as a result of the ongoing civil war and the inhumanities being perpetrated against civilians.
- Presenting to Parliament that UNAMIR could not stop any killing despite evidence to the contrary, thereby depriving the peacekeeping force of a strengthened mandate.
- Invoking Somalia and the 'Mogadishu factor' within the UNSC when arguing for a reduction of strength in UNAMIR's revised mandate, and thereby presenting the reduction as a rational decision.
- Predicating decision-making on Rwanda's civil war when there was clearly a parallel genocide occurring.
- Refusing, despite evidence to the contrary, to invoke the term 'genocide' in UNSC communications, on the advice of UK Government legal experts who concluded that such an admission would incur legal obligations in terms of the UNGC.
- Misrepresenting in Parliament the request made of the United Kingdom to provide troops and logistical support for the formation of UNAMIR II.
- Failing to dispatch with due haste the APCs that were desperately required to enable the launch of UNAMIR II and put a stop to genocide. The genocide was all but over before the APCs arrived in Rwanda.

In exploring this theme, it is evident that the objective of British foreign policy during the period concerned was not in keeping with those expected of a signatory to the UN Charter and the UNGC, and it must be suggested that such decision-making has neo-colonial underpinnings. Such policy is clearly incompatible with the British Government's legal obligations in terms of the UNGC and international law in general, and infers a degree of complicity in genocide by omission.

This case study further illuminates the implications of global elite bystander complicity in genocide for political ends and provides a clear indication of the direction in which criminology needs to take so as to move the boundaries of 'the genocide template' (Lemarchand 2006: 9). Whereas the micro study of France in Rwanda in Chapter 6 concluded that the knowing participatory role by the French was suggestive of complicity in genocide by assisting the perpetrators of the crime, this chapter concludes that the UK Government was responsible for complicity in genocide through crimes of omission, an act that amounts to a violation of international law. Arguably, as Robertson says, 'As for governments, realpolitik still rules when human rights comes up against superpowers interests' (2002: 533)

The politics of international law

In keeping with the scholarship of Bolewski, this research demonstrates that 'politics and law are not separate domains of international relations, but rather, they co-exist in a state of interdisciplinary cross-fertilization' (2007: 131). This is contradictory to the scholarship of Morgenthau (1985: 13), who maintains that politics is autonomous to the law. The approach undertaken in this book illuminates the complexities of how modern politics has conditioned the institution of international law. It further argues that international politics and law is a relationship of fascinating complexity and intrigue, a relationship that has evolved and finds expression in such diverse areas as complicity in genocide. Just as colonialism had a relationship to genocide, so do powerful political institutions, and that relationship cannot be 'understood as a one-off incident in which the criminal "event" is contained within a relatively narrow time frame' (Whyte 2009: 214). This study clearly establishes that the crime of global elite bystander complicity in genocide has a history. There is a history to the role taken by the French and the British in response to events in Rwanda; their violation of state responsibilities that are established in international law is clearly identifiable as part of an ongoing process of neo-colonial victimisation in central Africa that encompasses a sequence of events stretching over many years. Traditionally, criminology has been unhelpful in understanding crime as an ongoing process (Whyte 2007: 454) with power relationships between victims and offenders and the normalisation of being a repeat victim being misinterpreted by conventional criminologists (Walklate 2003: 127–9). Relationships between international politics and violations of international law can only be understood as part of an ongoing longitudinal process of unequal power relations.

This book approaches the concept of power in international politics from the perspective that powerful manipulation is not always readily visible, and by stripping away layers of complexity, we reveal how power operates in a multi-dimensional sense, influenced by the underlying precepts of economic and political advantage rather than human rights norms. That political decision-making, both before and during the genocide in Rwanda, was unhindered by legal obligations and reasoning, highlights the irrelevancy of international criminal law in politics, and its weak ability to prevent or resolve the incidence of genocide such as that in Rwanda.

One can therefore conclude that international criminal law is epiphenomenal to international politics, in that it manifests itself as all-powerful, but the reality is that when confronted with the actions of determined states, international criminal law becomes weak and ineffectual. This is in keeping with Bowring's characterisation of 'the degradation of international law' in the era since the US-led military attack on Iraq (2005: 245–9). Zolo argues that such discriminatory and discretionary adherence to international law is evident throughout history (2006, cited in Whyte 2009: 216); Toscano posits international law as an instrument of the dominant military and political actors, with 'consideration of the winners' crimes … systematically excluded' (ibid: 216). These views echo the allegations of the 'victor's justice' at the Nuremberg Trials.

Having clarified herein that international law is fundamentally political, with powerful institutions possessing the ability to influence and even create the law, it is evident that such legislation will not be upheld when it conflicts with the perceived political interests of the dominant states. International law is thus not enforceable independently of the will of powerful states, and one cannot regard it, in any compelling sense, as binding. As such, there needs to be a profound scepticism about law affording a viable path to international order. The ability of the British and French Governments to make political decisions in response to events in Rwanda for political and economic advantage was facilitated by their ability to break the law with impunity, a finding summarised by Whyte as one that 'is often treated as peripheral in criminology and socio-legal studies: that power is derived from the ability of the powerful to break the law' (2009: 218).

Motivations and opportunities

That international politics is a strategic game has evidenced itself in the roles played by both the French and UK Governments in seeking to maximise their respective political and economic interests within the existing international criminal constraints during the genocide in Rwanda. One has to understand that former colonial powers of Africa are in a constant pursuit of power. Indeed, a balance of power in the region is necessary for international stability, but this struggle does not justify the conduct of the United Kingdom and France before and during the Rwandan genocide of 1994.

Historical and contemporary rivalry is rooted in not only economic and geopolitical disputes over Africa, but also in mutual paranoia and a deep ideological and cultural division. That the behaviour of France and Britain in Rwanda in the period of the civil war from 1990 and throughout the genocide constituted an undeclared war between France and America, with Britain's foreign policy being driven by Washington, is a matter worthy of consideration.

It has become received wisdom in criminology that all crimes require motivation and opportunity. The motivation driving the French Government was reverberations of postcolonial global economics, as well as historical, political and ideological factors reminiscent from periods of colonisation. Rwanda's instability post-independence ensured that opportunities manifested themselves for powerful governments of the West to gain political control in the Great Lakes region of Africa, thereby providing an opportunity to manipulate the economic markets of Central Africa.

Chapter 8

A Conclusion

This research set out to explore the role of the British Government in Rwanda's genocide. The analysis presented reveals a lack of adherence to international law and concludes that Britain's role must be understood in the context of both colonialism, and political and economic advantage that is suggestive of neo-colonial underpinnings.

In the 18 years since the genocide in Rwanda, John Major's 1994 Government has repeatedly excused its decisions and actions in respect of Rwanda, claiming to have had no prior interest in the country and no access to intelligence or information. However, this study permits one to conclude that predicating their inaction on this basis is clearly inaccurate, especially since the United Kingdom's diplomatic relationships with France and Uganda ensured that the Government was well aware of events in Central Africa. This book demonstrates that the British Government *did* have knowledge that permitted a clear insight into the deteriorating conditions in Rwanda from 1990 onwards, and took a positive decision not to act to prevent genocide, thereby omitting to fulfil its obligations in terms of the UNGC and international law.

It was known that the GOR was supported militarily and ideologically, throughout the Presidency of Juvénal Habyarima, by the Government of France. However, it is only through the detailed research and analysis of this book that it is now evident that Kagame and the RPF were supported throughout, militarily and ideologically, by Britain and the United States. Such a revelation is of great importance since the ongoing crisis in the DRC that has seen the deaths of over 4 million people and untold crimes against humanity, is a direct consequence of the political instability in the Great Lakes region of Africa prompted by the RPF incursion into Rwanda in 1990, which led not only to the 1994 genocide but also to a refugee crisis in the then Zaire (Lemarchand 2009; Reyntjens 2011).

At the risk of being labelled a 'genocide negationist' or 'genocide revisionist' by the current Rwandan regime, a growing body of academics now challenge the official government genocide discourse (Straus and Waldorf 2011). Speculation has changed course repeatedly. Credible evidence indicates that an ICTR investigator, Michael Hourigan, learned in 1997 from various sources in Rwanda, that the RPF was responsible for the assassination of President Habyarimana, and that documentary evidence was available if required (see Deme 2010: 201 for the full affidavit of ICTR investigator Michael Hourigan, which was filed on 27 November 2006). This information was relayed to the Chief Prosecutor, Louise Arbour, who directed that no further action be taken[1] and the ICTR continued to focus its attention on allegations of crimes committed by Hutu extremists. Carla Del Ponte later replaced Arbour as Chief Prosecutor in 2003, and announced publicly her intention to pursue prosecution of the members of the Kagame regime for war crimes and crimes against humanity. Del Ponte was shortly thereafter replaced at the ICTR against her wishes; her long-term press aide states that she was removed from her position by the United States and United Kingdom owing to a long-standing political arrangement with the Kagame regime, which provided his regime with impunity for past and ongoing crimes in Central Africa (Hartmann 2007). ICTR defence lawyer Peter Erlinder, who was later arrested by the GOR for his criticism of the regime, indicates that the 'Rwanda genocide cover-up has been going on for at least a decade' (2008).

Since the formation of the post-genocide GOR, the United Kingdom has been one of the country's staunchest allies and is the its largest financial donor, unconditionally committing around £850m to date. And yet documentation reveals that by 17 May 1994, the United Kingdom and United States had knowledge that the RPF was responsible for mass killings and gross violations of human rights in Rwanda. Documentation from August, September and October 1994, which includes memos to US Secretary of State Warren Christopher, describes a conscious attempt by Western government officials to 'cover-up' reports of RPF killings (Adelman and Suhrke 2000). Between April and September 1994, the RPA massacred tens of thousands of civilians in what have been described as summary executions, giving rise to speculation of a double genocide (Prunier 1995). UN documents at the ICTR Military I trial suggest that 'US sponsored human rights reports by investigator Robert Gersony had documented massive military-style executions of civilians by Kagame's troops, during and after the final 90 days of the four year Rwanda war' from 1990 to 94 (Erlinder 2008). However, the current economy of Rwanda rests not only on international economic aid, but also on the plundering of the natural resources of the DRC, such as its diamonds and minerals (United Nations 2001), as well as permitting the trafficking through Rwanda of Angola's 'blood diamonds' on their way to Antwerp and beyond (Prunier 2009: 244).

Both Human Rights Watch and Amnesty International have documented mass rape, murder and other gross human rights abuses, resulting from the Rwandan presence in the DRC between November 1996 and May 1997. A recently drafted UN report documents the most serious violations of human rights and international humanitarian law committed within DRC territory between March 1993 and June 2003 (United Nations 2010). The report reveals more than 600 crimes, the majority of which have been committed by GOR forces headed by Kagame. It indicates that several of the crimes perpetrated by the Rwandan army in the DRC during the period of the study, 'point to circumstances and facts from which a court could infer genocidal intention' (ibid: 12). It alleges that the RPA, with the knowledge and support of Kagame, used hoes, bayonets and axes to massacre Rwandan and Congolese Hutus, and in many other cases the victims were raped, burned alive or shot dead (ibid).

Although Rwanda is a country where journalists and international lawyers face arrest, intimidation, harassment and violence, and human rights advocates are forced to flee the country for fear of persecution or arbitrary arrest, the British military has, throughout the past two decades, continued to provide unconditional training and strategic/tactical advice to Rwandan troops, in respect of the RPF's military incursions into the DRC. At a 2009 meeting between British Army chief General Sir Richard Dannatt and Kagame to discuss 'a number of issues regarding regional security', Dannatt advised Kagame that, 'We fully support what you are doing in securing peace and stability for this region, especially considering the negative influences in the Eastern part of the country [DRC] which pose a security threat to Rwanda' (Edmund 2009). Teresa Jones, Director of International Policy and Planning at the UK Ministry of Defence and Lieutenant Colonel Simon Etherington, the UK military attaché to Rwanda had in fact held a 'closed door meeting' with Rwandan Defence Minister General Marcel Gatsinzi on 26 January 2009 to discuss strengthening of UK–Rwanda bilateral military relationships and the ongoing Rwandan military offensive in Eastern DRC (The New Times 2009).

Whilst the United Kingdom and United States have persisted in their unwavering support of the RPF throughout the entire period of the genocide and beyond, the RPF has shrewdly created and sustained an overly simplified, RPF-politically correct view of the genocide and Rwandan history, for the consumption of the international community. This account of history debars any consideration of RPF responsibility for the genocide and reinforces how the United Nations and the West failed them, both before and during the genocide (Cameron 2003). The post-genocide RPF leadership became 'skilful masters of public relations and the art of disinformation' (Waugh 2004: 131), and Britain's support for Kagame and his government has undoubtedly provided the regime with integrative power in the form of legitimacy and respectability.

One of the key questions to be asked is whether the international community in general, but the United Kingdom in particular, is aware of the amount of illegal resource exploitation being undertaken by Rwanda in the DRC since the genocide?

Western governments have failed to be transparent regarding their role in the conflict in the DRC, preferring to obscure the involvement of their own multinational corporations in the illegal and illicit exploitation of the DRC's natural resources; 'once opened, the "closet" of illegal economic exploitation of the Congo has revealed the ugly head of militarized mercantilism'

(Nest 2006: 69). The permanent members of the UNSC established the Panel of Experts on the Illegal Exploitation of Natural Resources and Other Forms of Wealth of the Democratic Republic of Congo, which produced evidence that the GOR is actively involved in the illegal export of quantities of tin and tantalum to Asia (United Nations 2002). Tin plays a leading role in the upsurge in mineral exports from Rwanda, some of which is exported illegally and unlawfully. The country's total mineral export earnings in 2009 were more than $100m and were on course to exceed $200m in 2010. The other major export minerals from Rwanda are wolfram, coltan and gold.

When the aforementioned Panel delivered its reports (2001 and 2002), the United Kingdom downplayed the controversial recommendations, defending Rwanda and Uganda and rejecting all conclusions against them. As a result of the United Kingdom's reaction, the UNSC took no action and the international community has been left in a confused state. Evidence presented in these reports also indicate that the United Kingdom has sponsored Rwandan and Ugandan incursions into the Congo since 1996 for the purposes of the unlawful removal of valuable raw materials, and that British companies such as AFRIMEX facilitate this trade by importing minerals from the DRC via Rwanda (United Nations 2002).

These reports are further evidence that numerous British businesses, including Anglo American Plc, Barclays Bank and De Beers, have violated the Organisation for Economic Co-operation and Development guidelines for multinational enterprises (United Nations 2002). Corporations are influential international actors, with the ability to effect criminogenic behaviour of state organisations, and may therefore be usefully defined as global elite bystanders in terms of violations of international law. Corporations and states create liaisons because they often pursue the same objectives and often engage in unethical and illegal actions to achieve mutual goals (Michalowski and Kramer 2006). However, further research is required to develop a greater insight into the political economy of global elite bystander complicity in violations of international law, with a view to exploring the role and actions of corporations in such violations. By providing covert security, defence and strategic support to Rwanda, the United Kingdom *has* gained commercially from the many British corporations who have invested in the DRC's global mining industry, including the Anglo American subsidiary Anglo Gold Ashanti's gold mining operation in South Kivu. One must suggest that it is unproblematic for Western governments, with their own private geostrategic and monetary agendas, to inflame rather than solve the difficulties of states they earmark for political or military 'solutions' (Cameron 2010). Such findings also lead one to question whether the United Kingdom and United States waged the 1990–94 military offensive in Rwanda, using the RPF as a proxy to overthrow President Habyarimana, as a means to install a Government that was sympathetic to UK/US policies in Central Africa.

Reflections

Having explored the body of literature relating to the 'bystander', there is a clear need for the development of an enhanced academic understanding of the bystander in terms of violations of international criminal law, to include the powerful attributes of the global elite bystander whose geographical proximity to the location of the event is inconsequential in terms of culpability. To recap, the prerequisites for the global elite bystanders of this book are that the groups share the characteristics of a government, state, corporation, institution, international organisation, etc. They must possess power, authority, legitimacy and control to be part of the decision-making process. The groups should have the legitimacy to lead, and be in a position to influence the international community. Not all bystanders are equal, and any useful definition in respect of complicity in international crimes must acknowledge that some bystanders carry a greater responsibility than others.

In highlighting the legal standing in relation to global elite bystander complicity in genocide and other violations of international criminal law, the reader of this book is equipped with a lens to understand the scope of liability of states and other elite bystanders as responsible actors. Elite bystanders to genocide are, in sum, liable to charges of complicity in genocide should they fail to undertake their positive obligations, such as the prevention and suppression of acts of genocide or any of the other acts enumerated in Article III of the UNGC, where reliable intelligence clearly warned of imminent and serious humanitarian risks, and a clear moment of opportunity was identified but not acted upon. Establishing liability necessarily requires a determination of the effect that the global elite bystanders' non-compliance with their treaty obligations had on the perpetrators of genocide. Elite bystanders to genocide are also liable to charges of complicity in genocide should their actions be shown to have assisted, aided or abetted the perpetrators of genocide in some form. Article III makes punishable four forms of participation in the crime (conspiracy, direct and public incitement, attempt and complicity). This necessarily requires determination of the consequences for the perpetrators of genocide resulting from the assistance, aid and/or abetment provided by institutional bystanders. It must be proven that the global elite bystander had knowledge of the genocidal intent of the principal perpetrators, albeit they did not necessarily share that intent. These are the two key points of law relating to 'bystander' complicity (as opposed to direct involvement) in genocide that are of significance herein. By developing an external bystander's criminality in international law, our capacity to understand the role of the United Kingdom in the Rwandan genocide is enhanced. It also permits us to capture the nature of complicity of elite bystanders to genocide.

The role of France as a global elite bystander to genocide in Rwanda encompassed direct involvement and collusion with the genocidal Hutu regime, actions that were relatively overt, and which have been detailed elsewhere. In comparison, this book asserts that the British, as a global elite bystander to genocide in Rwanda, shaped conditions in the country every bit as much as the French, albeit their actions were much more hidden from scrutiny. These findings are useful in further developing the concept of global elite bystander complicity in genocide because one may even speculate that the covert, secretive activities and criminal complicity of the British Government is suggestive of an even greater degree of criminality than are the actions of the French. Academic discussions of state crime focus on overt acts such as military action, but this book identifies a form of state criminality that is hidden, and involves crimes of omission. Omission is only criminalised when there is a legal requirement imposing a clear obligation to act – as is found in Article I of the UNGC, which imposes an unconditional positive obligation on contracting parties to prevent genocide.

However, such legislated violations of international criminal law by states do not capture the equally important ongoing relationship between powerful political institutions and international law. Such relationships are relatively (if not completely) hidden, and encompass a series of deliberate acts in the furtherance of the political interests of dominant states over an extended period of time. What this book highlights are acts of state crime for which legislation is inappropriate owing to the weakness of that legislation, rather than the lack of recognition within legislation that the act is illegal. Such deviant conduct cannot be conceptualised under existing notions of state crime in international law, and as such, this research serves to illuminate the inadequacies and limitations of state crime in existent international law.

British Governments have long portrayed themselves as being rigorous in adhering to ethical principles; one former member of John Major's Cabinet stated when interviewed:

> We took great exception when Robin Cook became Foreign Secretary and said that he was going to launch an ethical foreign policy, for two reasons. First of all, it implied there had been no ethical dimension before, which was absurd, but secondly it implied that somehow ethics by themselves could determine foreign policy to the exclusion of other considerations. That just seems to me barking – it is just not deliverable.
> (Interview, London, 2006)

By way of explaining such contrasting behaviour, one can only speculate that since the British Government portrays British foreign policy as being underpinned by ethics, it is bound by necessity to use covert tactics when it undertakes activities that have clear non-ethical dimensions. Braithwaite (1999) has argued that shaming is the key to controlling all types of crime; exposure of such unethical decision-making policies within the bastion of the FCO and Cabinet Office would certainly be acutely embarrassing to the Government actors engaged in acts of complicity in violation of international law, and may be worthy of consideration as an appropriate method of confronting state crime. Such a suggestion is purely speculative, and detailed research is necessary to build on previous studies of controlling state crime in order to establish the viability of shaming, and to assess other appropriate methods of controlling such covert complicity in genocide.

It is also important to ask why the French Government was prepared to engage in complicity in genocide in a somewhat less secretive manner than the United Kingdom. France considers itself to be the birthplace of human rights, a tradition that can be dated back to the eighteenth century; indeed, France was one of the first nations to draft a declaration proclaiming human rights in 1789. However, France's relationship with the GOR, which was initiated in 1975 with the signing of the Franco–Rwandan agreement, has always been cloaked in the aspirations of human rights whilst concealing its real objectives of political and economic advantage in central Africa. Explanations of French military assistance to Rwanda at the behest of President Habyarimana, to repulse the invading RPF of 1990, were couched in human rights rhetoric; all subsequent overt and covert French military acts until the end of the genocide in July 1994 were also explained in these terms. Such justifications, of protecting the citizens of Rwanda against the invading rebel army of southern Uganda, empowered France to deny the criminality of its actions in violation of international law. Behaviour of this kind must be tackled by prosecution, thereby enforcing the international laws and conventions on genocide. It is in fact imperative that the French Government be held accountable by its informed constituencies for its complicit role in the genocide in Rwanda if future replications are to be deterred.

The international community's indifference to Rwanda brought tremendous embarrassment to the UNSC and the United Nations itself. In response to this failure, the then UN Secretary-General Kofi Annan urged the UN General Assembly to consider adopting a doctrine of humanitarian intervention. Canada sponsored an international commission, which after worldwide consultations proposed a 'responsibility to protect' (R2P) doctrine, suggestive a growing sense of mutual obligations. Under R2P, if a state cannot meet its obligations to protect its citizens, the international community inherits that responsibility. R2P has proven to be a useful instrument for human rights groups, activists and the domestic public in general, to indirectly pressure their state officials to act appropriately, and to hold those officials electorally accountable if they do not. The effectiveness of R2P in the international arena to combat behaviour by powerful institutions – which may include global elite bystander complicity in genocide – is as yet unproved.

Much criticism has been levelled at Western nations as a result of their inaction and response to the Rwandan genocide. However, to date, no studies have been undertaken to establish the responses and role of powerful African Governments both before and during the genocide of 1994 to establish if they too can be deemed as having been complicit, and if so, what was their motivation. The OAU (now the African Union, AU) consists of 54 African Heads of State. In 1998, the OAU established an independent Commission to investigate the 1994 genocide in Rwanda and the surrounding events in the Great Lakes region. The OAU and several African states, namely Tanzania, Uganda, Zaire and Burundi, played a central role in the Arusha Peace Accords, but the Commission's report was highly critical of the actions of this body (see UN Doc S/1999/1257), perceiving it as an active and vocal key actor during events in Rwanda, but like the United Nations, failing to define events in Rwanda as genocide. Neither did it call on the international community to treat the crisis accordingly (ibid). Instead, African leaders prefer to point fingers at the West. A criminological analysis of African states as global elite bystanders to the genocide in Rwanda and further research is essential to illuminate their role fully.

It is only once criminologists and international jurists can begin to piece together all elements of the tragedy and instability in the Great Lakes region throughout the past two decades that we will have a more realistic understanding of how international law might intervene to prevent a genocide like that which occurred in Rwanda from recurring in the future. This study is but one small step towards this objective in international law.

Notes

1 An Introduction

1 Taussig argues that '[c]annibalism acquired great ideological potency for the colonists from the beginning of the European conquest of the New World … it could be used to justify many policies including enslavement' (1984: 180). Mamdani states, 'It is more or less a rule of thumb that the more Western settlement a colony experienced, the greater was the violence unleashed against the native population' (2001: 10).
2 Republic of Zaire until 17 May 1997.
3 Author has complete set of documentation released by the FCO.

2 Global Elite Bystanders, Genocide Complicity and International Law

1 Despite a wealth of excellent scholarship on definitions, genocide remains a deeply contested concept with a lack of unanimity about its core definition (Charny 1999; Alvarez 2001; Straus 2001; Rittner *et al.* 2002; Kieran 2007). Despite widespread dissatisfaction amongst genocide scholars with the definition adopted by the 1948 UNGC (Chalk and Jonassohn 1990: 44–5), the document is useful in that it acts as a benchmark and an important place to begin a review of definitions.
2 Convention on the Prevention and Punishment of Genocide, Dec. 9, 1948, 78 U.N.T.S. 277, reprinted in *American Journal of International Law*, 45: 7 (1951).
3 Reservations to the Convention on the Prevention and Punishment of the Crime of Genocide (Advisory Opinion), [1951] I.C.J. REPORTS 16, at 21, quoted in Legality of the Treat or Use of Nuclear Weapons (Advisory Opinion), [1996] I.C. J. REPORTS 226, 31. See also Report of the Secretary-General pursuant to 2 of the Security Council Resolution 808 (1993), UN Doc S/25704, 45.
4 Prosecutor v. Goran Jelsic, Case No. IT-95-10-T, ICTY T. Ch. I, 14 Dec. 1999, para. 60.
5 Prosecutor v. Akayesu, Case No. ICTR-96-4-T, 2 Sep 1998.
6 The powers of the UNSC are as outlined in Chapter V(24) of the UN Charter (1945) and include the establishment of peacekeeping operations, peace-building/nation-building activities, international sanctions regimes and the authorization of military action, achieved by proposal of appropriate resolutions.
7 In accordance with the purposes and principles enshrined in the Charter of the United Nations, the Department of Peacekeeping Operations (DPKO) is dedicated to assisting the Member States and the Secretary-General in their efforts to

maintain international peace and security. 'The Department's [DPKO] mission is to plan, prepare, manage and direct UN peacekeeping operations, so that they can effectively fulfil their mandates under the overall authority of the Security Council and General Assembly, and under the command vested in the Secretary-General' (United Nations 2008b).

8 Peacekeeping forces are commonly referred to as 'blue helmets' or 'blue berets' because of their distinctive pale blue headwear.

9 For a full discussion on the relationship between humanitarian intervention and international law, see Tesón (1997); Gray (2000); Independent International Commission on Kosovo (2000); Chesterman (2001).

10 The circumstances and nature of humanitarianism have changed in recent years. The traditional ideals of neutrality, impartiality and independence have become myth. Rather than being at the margins of conflict, neo-humanitarianism is now embedded within contemporary conflict. States use humanitarian norms and actors for their own ends, frequently as a response to international pressure to intervene in conflicts. Such actions, as well as those on the part of international humanitarian organisations and other non-state actors, have altered the terrain of humanitarian action.

3 Reading the Histories of Rwanda

1 This land was referred to by the Europeans as Ruanda-Urundi, with Rwanda and Burundi being the traditional African names. Ruanda and Urundi are not a duality, though they have often been considered as one, and the term 'Ruanda-Urundi' refers merely to the geographical region of the two countries. 'Ruanda' and 'Urundi' have been used herein to describe events that occurred when those terms were being used by Europeans.

2 The branch of farming concerned with the cultivation of soil for the production of crops.

3 The branch of farming concerned with animal husbandry, and in this instance particularly the raising of cattle.

4 From November 1884 to February 1885, European countries met in Berlin, Germany, to divide Africa among themselves and to colonise the continent. The Berlin Conference coincided with Germany's sudden emergence as an imperial power.

5 In his major political analysis of the revolution Lemarchand (1970) compared 1959 Rwanda to 1789 France, and the revolutionaries to French Jacobins.

6 On 5 July 1973, the army commander, Juvénal Habyarimana seized power in Rwanda in a bloodless coup. He ordered many officials of the old regime killed, some after long periods of torture, but superstition prevented him sending his predecessor to the same fate. Instead he chose to surround Kayibanda's home with soldiers and starve him and his wife to death in captivity.

4 The Spectre of Genocide in Rwanda, and Its Aftermath: Internal and External Responsibility for Genocide

1 *Akazu* translates as a 'small house' of senior military and civilian officials, closely affiliated to the powerful clan of Agathe Habyarimana, the President's wife.

2 From 1990 to 1994, the RAF more than quadrupled, from 7,000 to 31,000 men, and purchased weaponry. See the Defence Intelligence Agency report written 9 May 1994, which is now declassified and available as 'Document 11' at http://www.gwu.edu/~nsarchiv/NSAEBB/NSAEBB53/rw050994.pdf

3 The name *Interahamwe* can be translated as 'Those who work together'. It was an extensive Hutu paramilitary organisation, supported by the Hutu GOR both

before and during the genocide, and its members were responsible for many deaths during the 1994 genocide.

4 The name *Impuzamugambi* means 'Those who have the same goal' or 'Those who have a single goal'. It was a small Hutu militia organisation, formed in 1992, and like the *Interahamwe*, it was responsible for many deaths during the 1994 genocide.

5 *Kangura* was a Rwandan magazine published in both Kinyarwanda and French, which published hate propaganda in the build up to the genocide of 1994. The magazine was launched in 1990 in response to the RPF-sponsored *Kanguka* magazine and the October invasion of Rwanda by the rebel RPF.

6 The Arusha Accords consisted of a Peace Agreement, the N'Sele Cease-Fire Agreement and two protocols plus earlier completed protocols governing the rule of law, power-sharing and the repatriation of refugees. See Letter from the Permanent Representative of the United Republic of Tanzania to the United Nations addressed to the Secretary-General, transmitting the Peace Agreement signed at Arusha on 4 August 1993, the N'Sele Cease-Fire Agreement and related Protocols of Agreement, UN Doc A/48/824-S/26915.

7 The fundamental difference between a Chapter VI and a Chapter VII mandate is the peacekeeping units' ability to use force. Under a Chapter VI mandate, peacekeepers can only use force in self-defence, while under a Chapter VII mandate they can be proactive in the use of force and indeed make peace if the situation warrants it. A Chapter VII mandate involves more risk to the peacekeeping contingents, because the likelihood of combat, and hence casualties, is higher; therefore the United Nations prefers Chapter VI mandates and its variations over Chapter VII mandates. Furthermore, VI Chapter mandates require the consent of all disputing factions, while Chapter VII mandates do not.

8 A UN observation force (UNOMUR) established in June 1993 to monitor the border between Rwanda and Uganda was folded into UNAMIR, although UNOMUR remained an autonomous body that kept its original mandate.

9 Herein, 'hardliners' refer to those exhibiting the doctrine, policy and posturing of a government or political body as being absolutist or authoritarian. The Hutu hardliner movement in Rwanda was and is extremist, militant, and uncompromising. As such, the term Hutu hardliner is interchangeable with Hutu extremism, Hutu Power and Hutu ruling elite.

10 Abdul Ruzibiza was a former officer and defector from Kagame's RPF, member of the crack unit known as the Network Commando and assigned to the French Department of Military Intelligence (DMI).

11 Testimony of Roméo Dallaire in Jean-Paul Akayesu's trial at the ICTR in Arusha Case No. ICTR-96-4-T.

12 A US-based Ugandan exile group.

13 For a detailed discussion on the negotiations that took place within Rwanda to secure another cease-fire after the outbreak of the genocide and civil war and the role of the UN in same, refer to Castonguay 2000: 271–80.

14 See Peterson 2001 for a clear and detailed account of the history to the civil strife in Somalia.

15 The Military I trial refers to the trial of Colonel Theoneste Bagosora, jointly accused with the former chief of operations of the former Rwandan army Brigadier Gratien Kabiligi, the former military commander of Gisenyi region, Colonel Anatole Nsengiyumva, and Major Aloys Ntabakuze, who was the commander of the Para-commando battalion based in Kanombe (Kigali).

16 This information is contained in a copy of a sworn affidavit of Michael Hourigan, investigator in Rwandan of ICTR, in possession of the author.

5 The French 'Resolution': 'Considerable Political and Geostrategic Interests are Hidden Behind the Rwandese Heap of Corpses'

1 See Dumoulin (1997) for a detailed discussion of French Military interventions and co-operation agreements in Africa.
2 Strategic raw materials are minerals that are vital to the functioning of high-technology industries. French dependency on Africa in 1985 was as follows: 100 per cent for cobalt, 87–100 per cent for uranium, 83 per cent for phosphates, 68 per cent for bauxite, 35 per cent for manganese and 32 per cent for copper.
3 The term 'Anglo-Saxon' is used to refer to the Anglophone peoples and societies of Britain, the United States and other countries such as Australia, Canada and New Zealand. It can be used in a variety of contexts often to identify the English-speaking world's distinctive language, culture, technology, wealth, markets, economy and legal systems.
4 Fashoda was the location of the climax to a series of territorial disputes between Britain and France. The 'Fashoda Syndrome' is the assertion of French influence in areas that may become susceptible to British influence.
5 Foccart (1913–97) spent much of his political career as the French chief adviser for African policy. He was considered the instigator behind various *coups d'état* in Africa during the 1960s.
6 See McCarthy (1987) for a detailed overview of the French left's accession to power.
7 See Human Rights Watch Arms Project (1994) for full details of the role of the French government in arming the perpetrators of genocide in Rwanda.
8 It is extremely difficult to get reliable estimates of numbers. This can be attributed to the conditions which the witnesses were facing. The disparity of witness estimates is evident in this transcript (see ICTR Case No ICTR-96-13).

6 Britain, Uganda and the RPF

1 One must acknowledge that a quantity of documentary evidence of significance to this book remains classified by the FCO.
2 Tony Wood, now deceased.
3 Cable, Kinshasa to London, 23 January 1991.
4 Cable from Kampala to London (FCO/HMC/17 – 1 October 1990).
5 Kampala to London (FCO/HMC/16 – 4 October 1990).
6 Ibid.
7 Ibid.
8 Kampala to London (FCO/HMC/15 – 8 October 1990).
9 Kampala to London (FCO/HMC/07 – 12 October 1990).
10 Kampala to London (FCO/HMC/12 – 1 November 1990).
11 Kinshasa to London (FCO/HMC/06 – 23 January 1991).
12 Kampala to London (FCO/HMC/11 – 24 January 1991).
13 Dar es salaam to London 1993 (FCO/HMC/25 – docs 14 October 1992 – 8 March 1993).
14 Oxfam Press Release, 22 January 1993, copy in possession of the author
15 Interview with former member of staff, British High Commission, Kampala, Uganda.
16 'Cockroach' is an offensive term used to refer to persons of Tutsi background, and was used as a form of dehumanization and neutralization.
17 Minister of State for Overseas Development 1989–97.
18 See Peterson (2001) for a basic introduction to events in Somalia October 1993 that led to the death of 18 US military rangers.

19 Copy of press release in possession of the author.
20 Copy of press release in possession of the author.
21 Copy of press release in possession of the author.
22 Copy of press release in possession of the author.
23 Copy of press release in possession of the author.
24 UN Resolution 912 dictated that UNAMIR should be reduced to 270 men with immediate effect, however General Dallaire refused to abide completely by this Resolution and retained a number of extra men.
25 Press Release by RPF 30 April 1994. Copy in possession of the author
26 Copy of letter obtained from Oxfam Archives and is in possession of the author
27 (PR/HMC/06 – 17 May 1994).
28 Copy of press release in possession of the author.
29 Copy of press release in possession of the author.
30 Copy of press release in possession of the author.

8 A Conclusion

1 The ICTR was dependent on the co-operation of the post-genocide GOR. Arbour was aware that it would ensure the mandate of the ICTR was terminated if crimes of the RPF were pursued by the court (Interview with Arbour, London, 2010).

Bibliography

Abiew, F.K. (1999) *The Evolution of the Doctrine and Practice of Humanitarian Intervention*, The Hague: Kluwer Law International

Adelman, H. and Suhrke, A. (1996) *The International Response to Conflict and Genocide: Lessons from the Rwanda Experience. Study 2: Early Warning and Conflict Management*, Copenhagen: Steering Committee of the Joint Evaluation of Emergency Assistance to Rwanda

——(2000) (eds.) *The Path of a Genocide: The Rwanda Crisis from Uganda to Zaire*, New Brunswick: Transaction Publishers

Africa Research Bulletin (2006) '*Rwanda-France: Diplomatic Relations Broken*', *Africa Research Bulletin: Political, Social and Cultural Series*, 43(11): 16877A–1687C

African Rights (1998) *Rwanda: Resisting Genocide. Bisesero April–June 1994*, London: African Rights

Agence France Presse (2008) 'Human Rights Watch Slams Rwanda for Blocking Senior Adviser', *AFP*, 24 December 2008

Aldrich, R. (1996) *Greater France: A History of French Overseas Expansion*, New York, NY: Palgrave

Alvarez, A. (2001) *Governments, Citizens, and Genocide: A Comparative and Interdisciplinary Approach*, Bloomington, IN: Indiana University Press

Amnesty International (1997) 'Rwanda: Ending the Silence', 23 September 1997. Available online at http://www.amnesty.org/en/library/info/AFR47/032/1997 [accessed 18 October 2006]

Annan, K. (2000) *We the People: The Role of the United Nations in the 21st Century*, New York, NY: United Nations

Assemblée Nationale, Mission d'Information Commune (1998) *Enquête Sur La Tragéédie Rwandaise (1990–1994)*, Paris: Assemblée Nationale, Dian-55/98

Barnett, M. (2002) *Eyewitness to a Genocide: The United Nations and Rwanda*, Ithaca, NY: Cornell University Press.

Barnett, V.J. (1999) *Bystanders: Conscience and Complicity during the Holocaust*, Westport, CN: Greenwood Press

Barouski, D. (2008) 'The International Criminal Tribunal for Rwanda Archive'. Available online at http://ebookbrowse.com/the-international-criminal-tribunal-for-rwanda-archive-by-david-barouski-pdf-d44123108

Bayart, J. (1995) 'Réflexion sur la politique africaine de la France', *Politique Africaine*, 58: 41–51

BBC Panorama (1995) 'The Bloody Tricolour', 20 August 1995

BBC Monitoring Africa (2009) 'Ugandan Presidential Aide Defends Boss Over Rwanda', 25 July 2009

Beres, L.R. (1989) 'Genocide, State and Self', in Friedrichs, D.O. (ed.) *State Crime, Vol II*, Aldershot: Ashgate

Bertrand, J. (2000) *Rwanda, le Piège de l'Histoire: l'Opposition Démoctrate Avant le Genocide 1990–1994*, Paris: Karthala

Betts, R.F. (1966) (ed.) *The "Scramble" for Africa: Causes and Dimensions of Empire*, Boston, MA: DC Heath and Co

Biddis, M.D. (1966) 'Gobineau and the Origins of European Racism', *Race*, 7: 255–70

Black, C. (2005) 'View from Rwanda: The Dallaire Genocide Fax: A Fabrication', Sanders Research Associates, http://www.sandersresearch.com, 1 December 2005

Blair, T. (1999) 'Doctrine of the International Community', speech to the Chicago Economic Club, 24 April 1999. Available online at http://www.number10.gov.uk/Page 1297 [accessed 11 January 2009]

Bolewski, W. (2007) *Diplomacy and International Law in Globalized Relations*, Danvers, MA: Springer

Bowring, B. (2005) 'The Degradation of the International Legal Order' in Whyte, D. (ed.) *Crimes of the Powerful: A Reader*, Maidenhead: McGraw-Hill

Braithwaite, J. (1999) *Crime, Shame and Reintegration*, Cambridge: CUP

Breitman, R. (1998) *Official Secrets: What the Nazis Planned, What the British and Americans Knew*, London: Penguin

Bridgman, J. and Worley, L. (2004) 'Genocide of the Hereros' in Totten, S., Parsons, W.S. and Charny, I.W. (eds) *Century of Genocide: Critical Essays and Eyewitness Accounts*, New York, NY: Routledge

Browning, C.R. (1993) *Ordinary Men: Reserve Police Battalion 101 and the Final Solution in Poland*, New York, NY: HarperCollins

Brownlie, I. (1963) *International Law and the Use of Force by States*, Oxford: OUP

Burkhalter, H. (1994) 'A Preventable Horror?', *Africa Report*, November–December 1994

Callamard, A. (2000) 'French Policy in Rwanda' in Adelman, H. and Suhrke, A. (eds) *The Path of a Genocide: The Rwanda Crisis from Uganda to Zaire*, New Brunswick, NJ: Transaction Publishers

Cameron, C. (2003) 'The Second Betrayal' Commemorating the 10th Anniversary of the Rwandan Genocide, Conference Paper, African Studies Association of Australalasia and the Pacific – Africa on a Global Stage. Available online at http://www.afsaap.org.au/Conferences/2003/Cameron.pdf [accesssed 13 October 2012]

Cameron, H. (2010) 'Britain's hidden role in Rwandan state violence', *Criminal Justice Matters*, 82(1): 18–20

——(2012) 'International Actor's and The Scramble for Congo's Riches', in Scarnecchia, T. and Flaschka, M.J. (eds) *Politics of Instability: Sexual Violence, Political Corruption, and International Complicity in the Democratic Republic of Congo*, Kent, OH: Kent State University Press [in press]

Castonguay, J. (2000) 'In search of a new cease-fire (April-July 1994)' in Adelman, H. and Suhrke, A. (eds) *The Path of a Genocide: The Rwanda Crisis from Uganda to Zaire*, New Brunswick, NJ: Transaction Publishers

Chalk, F. (2000) 'Hate Radio in Rwanda' in Adelman, H. and Suhrke, A. (eds) *The Path of a Genocide: The Rwanda Crisis from Uganda to Zaire*, New Brunswick, NJ: Transaction Publishers

Chalk, F. and Jonassohn, K. (1990) *The History and Sociology of Genocide: Analyses and Case Studies*, New Haven, CT: Yale University Press
Chambliss, W. (1989) 'State-Organised Crime', *Criminology*, 27(2): 183–208
Charbonnea, B. (2008) *France and the New Imerialism: Security Policy in Sub-Saharan Africa*, Aldershot: Ashgate
Charny, I.W. (1999) *Encyclopaedia of Genocide*, Santa Barbara, CA: ABC-Clio
——(2003) 'A Classification of Denials of the Holocaust and other Genocides', *Journal of Genocide Research*, 5(1): 11–34
Chesterman, S. (2001) *Just War or Just Peace? Humanitarian Intervention and International Law*, Oxford: OUP
Chomsky, N. (1999) *The New Military Humanism: Lessons from Kosovo*, London: Pluto Press
Chossudovsky, M. (2005) *The Globalization of Poverty and the New World Order*, Montreal: Centre for Research on Globalization.
——(2006) 'The Geopolitics behind Rwandan Genocide: Paul Kagame accused of War Crimes'. Available online at http://www.globalresearch.ca/index.php?context=va&aid=3958
Chrétien, J.P. (1985) 'Hutu et Tutsi au Rwanda et au Burundi', in Amselle, J.L. and M'Bokolo, E. (eds) *Au Coeur de l'Ethnie: Ethnies, Tribalisme et Etat en Afrique*, Paris, Editions La Decouverte
——(1995) *Rwanda: Les Medias du Genocide*, Paris: Karthala
Cohen, S. (2001) *States of Denial: Knowing About Atrocities and Suffering*, Cambridge: Polity Press
Cole, A. (1997) *François Mitterrand: A Study in Political Leadership*, London: Routledge
Coleman, R., Sim, J., Tombs, S. and Whyte, D. (2009) *State Power Crime*, London: Sage Publications
Collins, R. (1971) *Europeans in Africa*, New York, NY: Knopf
Cook, R. (2000) *Guiding Humanitarian Intervention*, speech given to the American Bar Association, 19 July 2000. Available online at http://www.fco.gov.uk/news/speechtext [accessed 5 December 2008]
Cooper, A.D. (2007) 'Reparations for the Herero Genocide: Defining the Limits of International Litigation', *African Affairs*, 106(422): 113–26
Coupland, R. (1967) *The Exploitation of East Africa, 1856–1890: The Slave Trade and The Scramble*, Evanston, IL: Northwestern University Press
Crosby, A. (1986) *Ecological Imperialism: The Biological Expansion of Europe 900–1900*, Cambridge: CUP
Curtis, M. (1998) *The Great Deception: Anglo-American power and world order*, London: Pluto
——(2003) *Web of Deceit: Britain's Real Role in the World*, London: Vintage
Dadrian, V.N. (2007) *The History of the Armenian Genocide: Ethnic Conflict from the Balkans to Anatolia to the Caucasus*, New York, NY: Berghan Books
Dallaire, R. (2004) *Shake Hands With the Devil*, Toronto: Random House Canada
Dedering, T. (1993) 'The German-Herero War of 1904: Revisionism of genocide or imaginary historiography?', *Journal of Southern African Studies*, 19(1): 80–8
Deme, A. (2010) *Rwanda 1994 and the Failure of the United Nations Mission*, Bloomington, IN: Xlibris Corp.
Derrida, J. (2001) *Writing and Difference*, London: Routledge

Des Forges, A. (1999) *Leave None to Tell the Story*, New York, NY: Human Rights Watch

Destexhe, A. (1995) *Rwanda and Genocide in the Twentieth Century*, New York, NY: New York University Press

Drechsler, H. (1980) *Let Us Die Fighting: The Struggle of the Herero and Nama Against German Imperialism (1884–1915)* [translated by Bernd Zöllner from *Südwestafrika unter deutscher Kolonialherrschaft, 1963*], London: Zed Press

Duignan, P. and Gann, L.H. (1975) *Colonialism in Africa, 1870–1960 (v.4)*, Cambridge: CUP

Dumoulin, A. (1997) *La France Militaire et l'Afrique. Coopération et Interventions: Un état de Lieux*, Brussels: Editions Complex

Edmund, K. (2009) 'Kagame, British Army Boss, Discuss Regional Security', *New Times Rwanda*, 12 February

Ehrenreich, R.M. and Cole, T. (2005) 'The Perpetrator-Bystander-Victim Constellation: rethinking Genocidal Relationships', *Human Organization*, 64(3): 213–24

Elder, T. (2005) 'What you see before your eyes: Documenting Raphael Lemkin's life by exploring his archival Papers, 1900–1959', *Journal of Genocide Research*, 7(4): 469–99

Eltringham, N. (2004) *Accounting for Horror: Post-Genocide Debates in Rwanda*, London: Pluto

Erlinder, P. (2008) 'Rwanda: No Conspiracy, No Genocide Planning … No Genocide?', *The Jurist: Legal News and Research*, 23 December 2008. Available online at http://jurist.law.pitt.edu/forumy/2008/12/rwanda-no-conspiracy-no-genocide.php [accessed 14 February 2009]

——(2009) 'The Real Authors of the Congo Crimes: Nkunda Has Been Arrested, But who Will Arrest Kagame', *Global research*, 2 February 2009, http://globalresearch.ca/index.php?context=va&aid=12139 [accessed 14 February 2009]

Evans, W.M. (1980) 'From the Land of Canaan to the Land of Guinea: The Strange Odyssey of the Sons of Ham', *American Historical Review*, 85: 15–43

Fein, H. (1993) *Genocide: A Sociological Perspective*, London: Sage

Fenn, E.A. (2000) 'Biological Warfare in Eighteenth Century North America', *Journal of American History*, 86(4): 1552–80

Foccart, J. and Gaillard, P. (1995/1997) *Foccart Parle: Entretiens Avec Philippe Gaillard*, Paris: Fayard

Frederick, A. (1910) *In the Heart of Africa*, London: Cassell and Company Ltd

French, H.W. (1996) 'France's army keeps grip in African ex-colonies', *New York Times*, 22 May

French Parliamentary Commission on Rwanda (1998) 'Report of the Information Mission of the National Defense and Armed Forces Committee and the Foreign Affairs Committee on the military operations led by France, other countries and the United Nations in Rwanda between 1990 and 1994', 15 December. Available online at http://www.assemblee-nationale.fr/dossiers/rwanda/rapport.asp [accessed 03 October 2012]

French Parliamentary Report (1999) *Par La Mission D'Information De La Commission De La Défense Nationale et Des Forces Armées et de la Commission Des Affaires Étrangeres: Su les opérations militaires menées par la France, d'autres pays et l'ONU au Rwanda entre 1990 et 1994*, Paris: Assemblée Nationale. Available online at http://www.assemblee-nationale.fr/dossiers/rwanda/r1271.asp [accessed 03 October 2012]

Friends of the Congo (2009) 'Congo-Kinshasa: Nkunda's "Arrest" and Rwanda's Response to International Pressure', *AllAfrica.com*, 6 February 2009, http://allafrica.com/stories/200902060607.html [accessed 03 October 2012]

Gaillard, P. and Barrada, H. (1994) 'The Story Direct from the Habyarimana Family', *Jeune Afrique*, 29 April, pp. 12–19
Gasana, K.J. (2002) *Rwanda: Du parti-État à l'État-garnison*, Paris: L'Harmattan
Gellately, R. and Kiernan, B. (2003) 'The Study of Mass Murder and Genocide' in Gellately, R. (ed.) *The Specter of Genocide: Mass Murder in Historical Perspective*, Cambridge: CUP
Gewald, J. (2004) 'Imperial Germany and the Herero of Southern Africa: Genocide-nad the Quest for Recompense', in Jones, A. (ed.) *Genocide, War Crimes & The West: History and Complicity*, London: Zed Books
Glaser, A. and Smith, S. (1994) *L'Afrique Sans Africains*, Paris: Stock
Goldhagen, D.J. (1996) *Hitler's Willing Executioners: Ordinary Germans and The Holocaust*, New York, NY: Knopf
Gorst, A. and Johnman, L. (1997) *The Suez Crisis*, Oxford: Routledge
Gould, J.S. (1981) *The Mismeasure of Man*, New York, NY: Norton
Gourevitch, P. (1998) *We Wish To Inform You That Tomorrow We Will Be Killed With Our Families: Stories from Rwanda*, New York, NY: Farrar, Straus and Giroux
——(2000) *We Wish To Inform You That Tomorrow We Will Be Killed With Our Families*, London: Picador
Gowan, P. (2001) 'Reviews', *New Left Review*, 8 Mar Apr 2001
Gray, C. (2000). *International Law and the Use of Force*, Oxford: OUP
Green, P. and Ward, T. (2004) *State Crime: Governments, Violence and Corruption*, London: Pluto
Gribbin, R.E. (2005) *In the Aftermath of Genocide: The U.S. Role in Rwanda*, New York, NY: iUniverse
Grogan, E. (1902) *From the Cape to Cairo: The First Traverse from South to North*, London: Hurst & Blackett
Hagan, J., Rymond-Richmond, W. and Parker, P. (2005) 'The Criminology of Genocide: The Death and Rape of Darfur', *Criminology*, 43(3): 525–61
Hammer, J. (2008) 'Soldier of good fortune: rebel leader Paul Kagame ended the Rwandan genocide. Has he also made that country a model for the rest of Africa?', *Washington Monthly*, 1 May
Hartmann, F. (2007) *Paix et chatiment: Les Guerres De La Politique*, Paris: Flammarion
Hilberg, R. (1992) *Perpetrators Victims Bystanders: the Jewish Catastrophe 1933–1945*, New York, NY: Harper Perennial
Hilsum, L. (1995) 'Reporting Rwanda: The Media and the Aid Agencies', Report prepared for *Joint Evaluation of Emergency Assistance to Rwanda, Study III* (1996, Vol. 3)
Hintjens, H. (1999) 'Explaining the 1994 Genocide in Rwanda', *The Journal of Modern African Studies*, 37(2): 241–86
Hochschild, A. (1999) *King Leopold's Ghost: A story of Greed, Terror and Heroism in Colonial Africa*, London: Macmillan
Hughes, G. (1996) 'The politics of criminological research', in Sapsford, R. (eds) *Researching Crime and Criminal Justice*, Milton Keynes: The Open University
Huliaras, A. (2003) '(Non)Policies and (Mis)Perceptions: The United States, France, and the crisis in Zaire', in Adelman, H. and Rao, G.C., *War and Peace in Zaire-Congo*, Trenton, NJ: Africa World Press
Hull, I.V. (2005), *Absolute Destruction: Military Culture and the Practices of War in Imperial Germany*, Ithaca, NY: Cornell University Press

Human Rights Watch (2008) 'End Bar on Human Rights Watch Staff Member', 23 December 2008. Available online at http://www.hrw.org/en/news/2008/12/23/rwanda-end-bar-human-rights-watch-staff-member [accessed 2 February 2009]

Human Rights Watch Arms Project (1994) 'Arming Rwanda: The Arms Trade and Human Rights Abuses in the Rwandan War', *Human Rights Watch*, 1 January 1994. Available online at http://www.unhcr.org/refworld/docid/3ae6a7fc8.html [accessed 27 March 2012]

Hurd, D. (2004) *Memoirs*, London: Abacus

Hutton, P. and Block, J. (2001) 'The Making of Idi Amin', *New African*. Available online at http://www.hartford-hwp.com/archives/36/502.html [accessed 27 March 2012]

Hyam, R. (1992) *The Labour Government and the end of Empire, 1945–1951*, London: HMSO

ICISS (2001a) *The Responsibility to Protect: Report of the International Commission on Intervention and State Sovereignty*, Ottawa: International Development Research Centre

——(2001b) *The Responsibility to Protect: Research, Bibliography, Background: Supplementary Volume to the Report of the International Commission on Intervention and State Sovereignty*, Ottawa: International Development Research Centre

ICTR Press Office (2008) 'Rwandan Military Leaders Found Not-Guilty of Conspiracy and Genocide Planning', ICTR-ADAD News Advisory, Post-Judgement News Conference, 18 December

Independent International Commission on Kosovo (2000) *The Kosovo Report: Conflict, International Response, Lessons Learned*, Oxford: OUP

International Law Commission (ILC) (1957) *Yearbook of the International Law Commission 1950, Vol II*, New York, NY: United Nations. Available online at http://untreaty.un.org/ilc/publications/yearbooks/Ybkvolumes(e)/ILC_1950_v2_e.pdf [accessed 27 March 2012]

——(1976) *Yearbook of the International Law Commission 1976, Vol II*, New York, NY: United Nations. Available online at http://untreaty.un.org/ilc/publications/yearbooks/Ybkvolumes(e)/ILC_1976_v2_p1_e.pdf [accessed 27 March 2012]

——(2001a) *Yearbook of the International Law Commission 2001, Vol I*, New York, NY: United Nations. Available online at http://untreaty.un.org/ilc/publications/yearbooks/2001.htm [accessed 03 October 2012]

——(2001b) 'Draft Articles on Responsibility of States for Internationally Wrongful Acts', report of 53rd Session (23 April–1 June and 2 July–10 August 2001). Available online at http://untreaty.un.org/ilc/texts/instruments/english/draft%20articles/9_6_2001.pdf [accessed 27 March 2012]

Johansson, P. (1995) 'International Press Coverage of the Rwanda conflict', report prepared for the Joint Evaluation of Emergency Assistance to Rwanda

Joint Evaluation of Emergency Assistance to Rwanda (1996) *The International Response to Conflict and Genocide: Lessons from the Rwanda Experience. Study 2: Early Warning and Conflict Management*, Copenhagen: Joint Evaluation of Emergency Assistance to Rwanda

Jorgensen, N.H.B. (2000) *The Responsibility of States for International Crimes*, Oxford: OUP

Kamukama, D. (1997) *Rwanda Conflict: Its Roots and Regional Implications*, Kampala: Fountain Press

Keane, Fergal (1996) *Season of Blood: Rwandan Journey*, London: Penguin

Kieran, B. (2007) *Blood and Soil: A World History of Genocide and Extermination from Sparta to Darfur*, New Haven: Yale University Press

Kiley, S. (1994) 'UN dithers on Rwanda rescue as Tutsi hail French troops', *The Times*, 27 June

Kisatsky, D. (2005) *The United States and the European Right, 1945–1955*, Columbus, OH: Ohio State University Press

Kittichaisaree, K. (2001) *International Criminal Law*, Oxford: OUP

Kramer, R.C. and Michalowski, R.J. (2005) 'War, Aggression and State Crime: A Criminological Analysis of the Invasion and occupation of Iraq', *British Journal of Criminology*, 45(4): 446–69

Kroslak, D. (2003) 'The Responsibility of Collective External Bystanders in Cases of Genocide: The French in Rwanda', in Erskine, T. (ed.) *Can Institutions Have Responsibilities? Collective Moral Agency and International Relations*, Basingstoke: Palgrave

——(2007) *The Role of France in the Rwandan Genocide*, London: Hurst & Company

Kuper, L. (1981) 'Genocide: Its Political Use in the Twentieth Century', in Hinton, A.L. (ed.) *Genocide: An Anthropological Reader*, Oxford: Blackwell

Kuperman, A.J. (2001) *The Limits of Humanitarian Intervention: Genocide in Rwanda*, Washington, DC: Brookings Institution

——(2004) 'Provoking Genocide: a Revised History of the Rwandan Patriotic Front', *Journal of Genocide Research*, 6(1): 61–84

Kwibuka, E. (2008) 'Des Forges Was Denied Entry as an Individual – Kalibata' *Rwanda New Times Rwanda*, 29 December

Lau, B. (1989) 'Uncertain certainties: The Herero-German War of 1904', *Mibagus*, 2: 4–5

Lemarchand, R. (1970) *Rwanda and Burundi*, London: Pall Mall Press

——(1994) 'The Apocalypse in Rwanda', *Cultural Survival Quarterly* (Summer/Fall): 29–39

——(1995) *Burundi: Ethnic Conflict and Genocide*, New York, NY: CUP

——(2004) 'The Rwanda Genocide', in Totten, S., Parsons, W.S. and Charny, I.W. (eds) *Century of Genocide: Critical Essays and Eyewitness Accounts*, New York, NY: Routledge

——(2006) 'Unsimplifying Darfur', in *Genocide Studies and Prevention*, 1(1): 1–12

——(2009) *The Dynamics of Violence in Central Africa*, Pennsylvania, PA: Pennsylvania Press

Leitenberg, M. (1994) 'Rwanda 1994: International Incompetence Produces Genocide', *Peacekeeping and International Relations*, 23(6): 6–10

Levene, M. (2005a) *Genocide in the Age of the Nation State, Vol I: The Meaning of Genocide*, London and New York, NY: IB Tauris

——(2005b) *Genocide in the Age of the Nation State, Vol II: The Rise of the West and the Coming of Genocide*, London and New York: IB Tauris

Livingston, S. and Eachus, T. (1995) 'US television Coverage of Rwanda', Study prepared for the Joint Evaluation of Humanitarian Assistance to Rwanda, Study II (Vol. 2, 1996)

——(2000) 'Rwanda: U.S. Policy and Television Coverage', in Adelman, H. and Suhrke, A. (eds) *The Path of a Genocide: The Rwanda Crisis from Uganda to Zaire*, New Jersey, NY: Transaction Publishers

Louis, W.R. (1963) *Ruanda-Urundi 1884–1919*, Oxford: Clarendon Press.

——(2006) *End of British Imperialism: The Scramble for Empire, Suez and Decolonization*, London and New York, NY: IB Tauris

Luckham, R. (1982) 'French militarism in Africa', *Review of African Political Economy*, 9(24): 55–84

Madsen, W. (1999) *Genocide and Covert Operations in Africa 1993–1999*, Lampeter: Edwin Mellen Press Ltd

Malone, D. (2004) *The UN Security Council: From the Cold War to the 21st Century*, London: Lynne Rienner

Mamdani, M. (2001) *When Victims Become Killers: Colonialism, Nativism, and the Genocide in Rwanda*, Princeton, NJ: Princeton University Press

Mann, Michael, (2005) *The Dark Side of Democracy: Explaining Ethnic Cleansing*, Cambridge: CUP

Martin, G. (1985) 'The Historical, Economic, and Political Bases of France's African Policy', *Journal of Modern African Studies*, 23(2): 189–208

——(1995) 'Continuity and Change in Franco-African Relations', *Journal of Modern African Studies*, 33(1): 1–20

McCarthy. P. (1987) *The French Socialists in Power, 1981–1986*, Westport, CT: Greenwood Press

McDonnell, M. and Moses, A.D. (2005) 'Raphael Lemkin as historian of genocide in the Americas', *Journal of Genocide Research*, 7(4): 501–29

McGreal, C. (2007) 'France's Shame?', *The Guardian, G2 Features*, 11 January, p. 10

McIntosh, A. (1997) 'Rwanda Beyond Ethnic Conflict', *Development in Practice*, 7(4): 464–74

McNulty, M. (2000) 'French arms, war and genocide in Rwanda', *Crime, Law and Social Change*, 33(1): 105–29

McQueen, C. (2005) *Humanitarian Intervention and Safety Zones: Iraq, Bosnia and Rwanda*, Basingstoke: Palgrave MacMillan

Melvern, L. (2000) *A People Betrayed: The Role of the West in Rwanda's Genocide*, London: Zed Books

——(2004) *Conspiracy to Murder: The Rwandan Genocide*, London: Verso

——(2008) 'Essay: The Perfect Crime', *Prospect*, February

Memmi, A. (1991) *The Colonizer and the Colonized*, Boston, MA: Beacon Press

Meredith, M. (2005) *The State of Africa: A History of Fifty Years of Independence*, London: Free Press

Merivale, H. (1861) *Lectures on Colonization and Colonies*, London: Green, Longman and Roberts

Meyer, H. (1916) *Die Barundi: Eine völkerkundliche Studie aus Deutsch-Ostafrika*, Leipzig: Otto Spamer

Michalowski, R.J. and Kramer, R.C. (2006) 'The Critique of Power', in Michalowski, R.J. and Kramer, R.C. (eds.) *State-Corporate Crime: Wrongdoing at the Intersection of Business & Government*, London: Rutgers University Press

Mills, K. (2005) 'Neo-Humanitarianism: The Role of International Humanitarian Norms and Organizations in Contemporary Conflict', *Global Governance*, 11(Apr–Jun): 161–83

Mingst, K. and Karns, M.P. (2000) *The United Nations in the Post-Cold War Era*, Boulder, CO: Westview Press

Mingst, K.A. and Karns, M.P. (2007) *United Nations in the Twenty First Century*, Boulder, CO: Westview Press

Morel, E. (1905) *King Leopold's Rule in Africa*, New York, NY: Funk and Wagnalls

Morgenthau, H.J. (1985) *Politics Among Nations: The Struggle for Power and Peace*, New York, NY: McGraw-Hill

Moses, A.D. (2000) 'An Antipodean Genocide? The Origins of the Genocidal Moment in the Colonisation of Australia', *Journal of Genocide Research*, 2(1): 89–106

Mucyo Commission Report (2008) *Commission Nationale Independandte Chargee De Rassembler Les Preuves Montrant L'Implication De L'Etat Francais Dans Le Genocide Perpetre Au Rwanda En 1994*, Government of Rwanda, 15 November 2007. Available online at http://www.aidh.org/rwand/Images/RAPPORT-MUCYO.pdf [accessed 03 October 2012]

Mupenzi, C. (2006) 'French soldiers blamed for Bisesero killings', *The New Times Rwanda*, 17 December

Mutibwa, P. (1992) *Uganda Since Independence: A Story of Unfulfilled Hopes*, London: Hurst & Co/Trenton, NJ: Africa World Press

Nest, M. (2006) *The Democratic Republic of Congo: Economic Dimensions of War and Peace*, Boulder, CO: Lynne Rienner

New Times, The (2009) 'Gen. Gatsinzi Receives UK Defence Officials', 27 January, Kigali, Rwanda

Newbury, C. (1988) *The Cohesion of Oppression: Clientship and Ethnicity in Rwanda, 1860–1960*, New York, NY: Columbia University Press

——(1978) 'Ethnicity in Rwanda: The Case of Kinyaga', *Africa*, 48(1): 17–29

Newbury, D. (2011) 'The Historian as Human Rights Activist', in Straus, S. and Waldorf, L. (eds) *Remaking Rwanda: State Building and Human Rights After Mass Violence*, Madison, WI: University of Wisconsin Press

Nkrumah, K. (1965) *Neo-Colonialism: The Last Stage of Imperialism*, London: Thomas Nelson & Sons

Nkundabagenzi, F. (1961) *Le Rwanda politique (1958–1960)*, Brussels: CRISP

Nundy, J. (1994) 'Balladur Takes a Moral Stance on Intervention', *The Independent*, 23 June

Nzongola-Ntalaja, G. (2005) *From Zaire to the Democratic Republic of the Congo*, Uppsala: Nordiska Afrikainstitutet

Ó Gráda, C. (1999) *Black '47 and beyond: The Great Irish Famine in History, Economy and Memory*, Princeton, NJ: Princeton University Press

Oliver, R.A., Fage, J.D. and Sanderson, G.N. (1985) *The Cambridge History of Africa*, Cambridge: CUP

Organization of African Unity (OAU) (2000) *Rwanda: The Preventable Genocide*. Available online at http://www.visiontv.ca/RememberRwanda/Report.pdf [accessed 1 February 2005]

Otunnu, O. (2000) 'An Historical Analysis of the Invasion by the Rwandan Patriotic Front', in Adelman, H. and Suhrke, A. (eds) *The Path of a Genocide: The Rwanda Crisis from Uganda to Zaire*, New Jersey: Transaction Publishers, pp. 31–49

Pakenham, T. (1992) *The Scramble for Africa*, London: Abacus

Pééan, P. (2005) *Noires Fureurs, Blancs Menteurs*, Paris: Mille et Une Nuits

Peterson, S. (2001) *Me Against My Brother: At War in Somalia, Sudan and Rwanda*, New York, NY: Routledge

Pfaff, William, (1998) 'An active French role in the 1994 genocide in Rwanda', *The International Herald Tribune*, 17 January, p. 24

Philipps, J.E.T. (1923) ' "Mufúmbiro": The Birunga Volcanoes of Kigezi-Ruanda-Kivu', *The Geographical Journal*, 61(4): 233–53

Philpot, R. (2004) *Rwanda 1994: Colonialism Dies Hard.* Available online at http://www.taylor-report.com/Rwanda_1994 [accessed 16 March 2012]

——(2005) *Ca ne s'est pas passéé comme ça à Kigali*, Montreal, QC: Les Editions des Intouchables

Pottier, J. (2002) *Re-imagining Rwanda: conflict, survival and disinformation in the late 20th century*, Cambridge: CUP

Power, S. (2002) *"A Problem From Hell": America and the Age of Genocide*, London: Flamingo

Prunier, G. (1995/2002) *The Rwandan Crisis: History of a Genocide*, London: Hurst & Company

——(1998) 'The Rwandan Patriotic Front', in Clapham, C. (ed.) *African Guerillas*, Bloomington, IN: Indiana University Press

——(2009) *From Genocide To Continental War: The Congolese Conflict and the Crisis of Contemporary Africa*, London: Hurst & Company

Public Records Act (1958) *The National Archives.* Available online at http://www.nationalarchives.gov.ac/policy/act [accessed 2 June 2006]

Pugh, M. (1999) *Britain Since 1789: A Concise History*, New York, NY: Palgrave

Quigley, J. (1986) 'Complicity in international law: A new direction in the law of State responsibility', *British Yearbook of International Law, Vol. 57*, pp. 77–131

Reyntjens, *F. (* 1994) *L'Afrique des Grands Lacs en Crise: Rwanda, Burundi: 1988–94*, Karthala: Paris

——(1995) *Trois jours qui ont fait basculer l'histoire*, Paris et Tervuren: L'Harmattan et Institut Africain-CEDAF

——(2004) 'Rwanda, ten years on: From genocide to dictatorship', *African Affairs*, 103(411): 177–210

——(2011) 'Constructing the Truth, Dealing with Dissent, Domesticating the World: Governance in Post-Genocide Rwanda', *African Affairs*, 110(438): 1–34

Rittner, C., Roth, J.K. and Smith, J.M. (2002) *Will Genocide Ever End?*, St Paul, MN: Paragon House

Robertson, G. (2002) *Crimes Against Humanity: The Struggle for Global Justice*, London: Penguin

Ruzibiza, A.J. (2005) *Rwanda: L'Histoire Secrète*, Paris: Editions du Panama

Ryan, L. (1996) *The Aboriginal Tasmanian*, Crows Nest: Allen and Unwin Pty Ltd

Saint-Exupéry, P. (1998a) 'France-Rwanda; un genocide sans importance', *Le Figaro*, 12 January

——(1998b) 'Des Silences d'Etat', *Le Figaro*, 14 January

——(2004) *L'inavouable: La France Au Rwanda*, Paris: Les arènes

Sale, K. (1990) *The Conquest of Paradise: Christopher Columbus and the Columbian Legacy*, New York, NY: Knopf

Sanders, E. (1969) 'The Hamitic Hypothesis; It Origin and Functions in Time Perspective', *Journal of African History*, 10: 521–3

Sarkin, J. (2009) *Colonial Genocide and Reparations Claims in the 21st Century: The Socio-Legal Context of Claims under International Law by the Herero against Germany for Genocide in Namibia, 1904–1908*, Westport, CT: Praeger Security International

Schabas, W.A. (2000) *Genocide in International Law*, Cambridge: CUP

Schaller, D.J. (2005) 'Raphael Lemkin's view of European colonial rule in Africa: between condemnation and admiration', *Journal of Genocide Research*, 7(4): 531–8

Schraeder, P.J. (2000) 'Cold War to Cold Peace: Explaining U.S.-French Competition in Francophone Africa', *Political Science Quarterly*, 115(3): 395–419

Schwendinger, H. and Schwendinger, J. (1975) 'Defenders of Order or Guardians of Human Rights', in Taylor, I., Walton, P. and Young, J. (eds) *Critical Criminology*, London: Routledge and Kegan Paul.

Shaw, M. (2003) *International Law*, 5th edition, Cambridge: CUP

Simon, D.R. (2002) *Elite Deviance*, Boston, MA: Pearson Education

Sirven, P., Gotanègre, J.F. and Prioul, G. (1975) *Géographie du Rwanda*, Brussels: A. De Bock

Smith, S. (1994) 'Afrique Noir: Le Duel Washington-Paris', *Politique Internationale*, 63: 355–67

Stanley, H.M. (1878) *Through the Dark Continent: Or the Sources of the Nile Around the Great Lakes of Equatorial Africa and Down the Livingstone River to the Atlantic Ocean*, London: Sampson Low, Marston, Searle & Rinigton

Stannard, D. (1992) *American Holocaust: The Conquest of the New World*, New York, NY: Oxford University Press

Stanton, G.H. (2004) 'Could the Rwandan Genocide Have Been Prevented', *Journal of Genocide Research*, 6(2): 211–28

——(2005) *Encyclopedia of Genocide and Crimes Against Humanity*, Farmington Hills, MI: Thomson-Gale

Stettenheim, J. (2000). 'The Arusha Accords and the Failure of International Intervention in Rwanda', in Greenberg *et al.*, *Words over Water: Mediation and Arbitration to Prevent Deadly Conflict*, New York, NY: Carnegie Commission on Preventing Deadly Conflict

Stevenson, J. (1995) *Losing Mogadishu: Testing U.S. Policy in Somalia*, Annapolis, MD: Naval Institute Press

Stohl, M. (1987) 'Outside of a Small Circle of Friends: States, Genocide, Mass Killing and The Role of Bystanders' *Journal of Peace Research*, 24(2) 151–66

Straus, S. (2001) 'Contested meanings and conflicting imperatives: a conceptual analysis of genocide', *Journal of Genocide Research*, 3(3): 349–75

——(2006) *The Order of Genocide: Race, Power, and War in Rwanda*, Ithaca, NY: Cornell University Press

——and Waldorf, L. (eds) (2011) *Remaking Rwanda: State Building and Human Rights After Mass Violence*, Madison, WI: University of Wisconsin Press

Taussig, M. (1984) 'Culture of Terror – Space of Death: Roger Casement's Putumayo Report and the Explanation of Torture', *Comparative Studies in Society and History*, 26(3): 467–97

Taylor, I. (2003) 'Conflict in Central Africa: Clandestine Networks & Regional/ Global Configurations', *Review of African Political Economy*, 30(95): 45–55

——(2010) *The International Relations of Sub-Saharan Africa*, New York, NY: Continuum

Tesón, F.R. (1997) *Humanitarian Intervention: An Inquiry into Law and Morality*, 2nd edition, Dobbs Ferry, NY: Transnational Publishers

Thomas, H. (1999) *The Slave Trade: the Story of the Atlantic Slave Trade, 1440–1870*, London: Simon & Schuster

Thomas, N. (1994) *Colonialism's Culture: Anthropology, Travel and Government*, Cambridge: Polity Press

Todorov, T. (1996) *Facing The Extreme*, New York, NY: Metropolitan Books

Tuck, R. (1999) *The Rights of War and Peace: Political Thought and the International Order From Grotius to Kant*, Oxford: OUP

Turner, T. (2007) *The Congo Wars*, London, Zed Books

Tyler, P.E. (1994) 'North Korea Bars A-Plant Survey', *The New York Times*, 21 March

United Nations (1945) *Charter of the United Nations*. Available online at http://www.un.org/aboutun/charter [accessed 5 December 2008]

——(1948) *Charter of the United Nations*. Available online at http://www.un.org/aboutun/charter [accessed 5 December 2008]

——(2001) 'Report of the Panel of Experts on Illegal Exploitation of Natural Resources and Other Forms of Wealth of the Democratic Republic of the Congo', Report of the Panel of Experts, Geneva, UN Doc S/2001/1146

——(2002) 'Report of the Panel of Experts on Illegal Exploitation of Natural Resources and Other Forms of Wealth of the Democratic Republic of the Congo', Report of the Panel of Experts, United Nations, Geneva, UN Doc S/2002/1146

——(2003) 'Report of the Panel of Experts on Illegal Exploitation of Natural Resources and Other Forms of Wealth of the Democratic Republic of the Congo', Report of the Panel of Experts, United Nations, Geneva, UN Doc S/2003/1146

——(2008a) Final Report of the Group of Experts on the Democratic Republic of Congo, United Nations, Geneva, UN Doc S/2008/773

——(2008b) *Department of Peacekeeping, Mission Statement, Peace and Security Section*, United Nations Department of Public Information

——(2010) Democratic Republic of the Congo, 1993–2003: Report of the mapping exercise documenting the most serious violations of human rights and international humanitarian law committed within the territory of the Democratic Republic of the Congo between March 1993 and June 2003, Office of the High Commissioner for Human Rights, United Nations

United Nations Development Programme (2007) *Turning Vision 2020 Into Reality: From Recovery to Sustainable Human Development*. Available online at http://hdr.undp.org/en/reports/nationalreports/africa/rwanda/RWANDA_2007_en.pdf [accessed 24 March 2012]

United Nations Genocide Convention (1948) *United Nations Genocide Convention*. Available online at http://www.hrweb.org/legal/genocide.html [accessed 20 November 2004]

United Press International (2008) 'UN's Louise Arbour Under Fire Over Rwanda by UPI', 9 April. Available online at http://www.upi.com/Official_Government_Wires/Story/20080409-055109-7508/ [accessed 09 December 2009]

Valier, C. (2005) 'Complicity and The Bystander To Crime', A paper presented in the Centre for the Study of Law and Society Bag Lunch Speaker Series, University of California, Berkley. Available online at http://repositories.cdlib.org/cgi/viewcontent.cgi?article=1067&context=csls [accessed 09 December 2009]

Verrier, A. (1983) *Through the Looking Glass: British Foreign Policy in an Age of Illusions*, London: Jonathan Cape

Vidal, C. (1969) 'Le Rwanda des Anthropologies ou le Féétichisme de la Vache', *Cahiers d'Etudes Africaines*, 9(3): 384–401

Waldorf, L. (2011) '"A Mere Pretense of Justice": Complementarity, Sham Trials, and Victor's Justice at the Rwanda Tribunal', *Fordham International Law Journal*, 33(4): 1221–1277

Walklate, S. (2003) *Understanding Criminology: Current Theoretical Debates*, Maidenhead: McGraw-Hill

Wallis, A. (2006) *Silent Accomplice: The Untold Story of France's Role in Rwandan Genocide*, London: IB Tauris

Walters, R. (2003) *Deviant Knowledge*, Cullompton, Cullompton: Willan Publishing

Watt, I.P. (1979) *Conrad in the Nineteenth Century*, Berkeley and Los Angeles, CA: University of California Press

Waugh, C. (2004) *Paul Kagame and Rwanda: Power, Genocide, and the Rwandan Patriotic Front*, Jefferson, NC: McFarland and Company

Wayland, E.J. (1921) 'Some Account of the Geology of the Lake Albert Rift Valley', *The Geographical Journal*, 58(5): 344–59

Weiss, T.G. (2004) 'The Humanitarian Impulse', in Malone, D.M. (ed.) *The UN Security Council: From the Cold War to the 21st Century*, Boulder, CO: Lynne Rienner Publishers

Welsh, J. (2008) 'The Security Council and Humanitarian Intervention', in Lowe V., Roberts, A. and Zaum, D. (eds), *The United Nations Security Council and War*, Oxford: OUP

Wertheim, S. (2010) 'A Solution from Hell: The United States and the Rise of Humanitarian Interventionism, 1991–2003', *Journal of Genocide Research*, 12(3–4): 149–72

——(2011) 'On Moralism and Rwanda: A Reply to Linda Melvern', *Journal of Genocide Research*, 13(1–2): 159–63

Wheeler, N.J. (2000) *Saving Strangers: Humanitarian Intervention in International Society*, Oxford: OUP

Whyte, D. (2007) 'Victims of Corporate Crime', in Walklate, S. (ed.) *Handbook of Victims and Victimology*, Uffculme: Willan

——(2009) 'The Power to Break the Law', in Whyte, D. (ed.) *Crimes of the Powerful: A Reader*, Maidenhead: McGraw-Hill

Williams, K. (1989) 'Researching the powerful: Problems and possibilities of social research', *Contemporary Crises*, 13: 253–74

Woodhouse, C.M. (1962) *British Foreign Policy Since the Second World War*, London: Huchinson

World Bank (1994) *Rwanda: Poverty Reduction and Sustainable Growth*, Report No. 12465-Rwanda, 16 May

Yacoubian, G.S. (2000) 'The (In)significance of Genocidal Behavior to the Discipline of Criminology', *Crime, Law and Social Change*, 34(1): 7–19

Zolo, D. (2002) *Invoking Humanity: War, Law and Global Order*, London: Continuum

Index

Please note that page numbers relating to Notes will have the letter 'n' following the page number.